Adoption is Forever

*Two perspectives on the love,
heartache and hope of the journey toward choice,
family and fulfillment*

Rhonda Pollero & Traci Hall

Wyatt-MacKenzie Publishing, Inc.
DEADWOOD, OREGON

Adoption is Forever

Two perspectives on the love, heartache and hope of the journey
toward choice, family and fulfillment

by Rhonda Pollero, Traci Hall

FIRST EDITION

ISBN: 978-1-932279-89-4

Library of Congress Control Number 2008940956

Edited by Bonnie Crisalli

W

Wyatt-MacKenzie Publishing, Inc.
DEADWOOD, OREGON

Wyatt-MacKenzie Publishing, Inc., Deadwood, OR
www.WyMacPublishing.com (541) 964-3314

Requests for permission or further information should be addressed to:
Wyatt-MacKenzie Publishing, 15115 Highway 36, Deadwood, Oregon 97430

INTRODUCTION

This could have been the most challenging part of writing this book until Traci and I decided it would be a good idea for us to introduce each other. After all, this project was one-hundred percent collaboration. I moved to Florida five years ago and other than relatives, didn't know a soul. I knew as a professional writer I could find a community and begin to build friendships. Call it Karma, Fate—whatever, but one of the first people I met was Traci Hall. Given that the writers meetings were an hour-plus drive from our homes, we had time to get to know one another. I think by our third road trip, I was spilling my guts about my son Kyle, who had died, and my beautiful Katie Scarlett whom we adopted from Russia. Traci then shared with me that she'd been a young teenage mother who had opted for an open adoption plan for her baby. She was the first birth mom I'd ever known. Though I didn't say it aloud, I was in awe. It takes a selfless person to surrender their child to another family, even the family she'd hand-picked to raise her child. I was surprised at the guilt she carried with her, though I understood some of it. Even though I intellectually know I couldn't have done anything to save my son's life, I still feel guilty that I couldn't save him.

Over the next year or so we began to talk more about our adoption experiences and all the misconceptions people have about the adoption process. The fact that we share a wicked sense of humor helped us shape how we wanted to share our respective journeys. Our goal was to inform but to do so with honesty and humor. Some topics will make you cry, others (hopefully) will have you laughing. And this book was born. It is amazing how many of the same emotions we experienced even though we were on opposite sides of the adoption process. I'm a better person for having Traci in my life. She's given me insights that have served me well as my daughter ages and asks me questions about her birth mother. Listening to and reading Traci's story reminds me that I owe my daughter's birth mother a huge debt of gratitude.

Meeting Rhonda changed my life in so many ways. She is a dynamic, intelligent woman who manages to do more in twenty-four hours than anybody else I know. I think she made a deal with Someone Important and got extra hours in her day. She took me under her wing almost five years ago, and has since guided me through the minefield of publishing.

Not to be cliché, but without Rhonda, this book never would have been written. The subject of adoption can be a sensitive one, and in my case, I carried a lot of residual guilt. I never hid the fact that I'd given a child up for adoption— but I didn't exactly wave the information around on a red flag, either. On one of the many drives to and from our writer's meetings, she shared that her daughter Katie was adopted, and why. Astounded at her trust, I told my adoption story. She didn't judge me, and she didn't give me platitudes. I adored her. Later, we discussed collaborating on a book about adoption, from both viewpoints—the adoptive mother, and the birth mother. We wanted to share our journeys and show the world that adoption can be a fulfilling, viable option for a family unit. Rhonda gave me the nudge I needed to forgive the impetuous teenager I'd been in my youth, and embrace the grown-up me who is a fine person in spite of herself. Rhonda has faced challenges in her life that would slay a lesser person, and yet she's got a killer sense of humor as well as a generous nature. I am very, very proud to call her my friend.

We would be remiss if we didn't include Nancy Cleary, publisher of Wyatt-MacKenzie. She believed and supported this project from the beginning. She realized that most books on adoption were either 'how-tos' or 'happily-ever-after' testaments, so there was a need this book would meet both for birth mothers contemplating adoption and adoptive parents considering building their family through adoption.

We intentionally chose Bonnie Crisalli as our editor. Rhonda has a long history with Bonnie, she was her second editor and their friendship dates back to the early 1990s. Bonnie also happens to be an adoptive mother but her story is quite different and included as an Editor's Note at the end of the book.

Lastly, this has been a true labor of love for both Traci and Rhonda. One we could not have conquered without the support of our spouses and children; our devoted editor; our supportive publisher; and each other.

A REVIEW

From the Adoptive Parents

"This book offers a raw viewpoint of a birth mothers side of an open adoption, and gives insight into the birth mothers many struggles and human emotion that extends to all the parties involved. As open adoptive parents who already knew much of the story but not from Traci's viewpoint, it brought tears to our eyes.

We didn't know anything about open adoption at the time, we just went with our gut feelings and made up the rules as we went along. We can see now how much TRUST on both sides was present and that our support system of mothers, aunts and even Kasey helped us through the process.

I recommend this book to anyone wanting to learn more about open adoption, and explore the possibilities and outcomes, the rewards and a chance to find out about your-self in the process. This human story should be one of those made for television Movies of the Week, at least.

Thank You for taking the time to tell the story Traci and for you and your family being a part of our lives."

~ Dee and Garth

TABLE OF CONTENTS

Rhonda Pollero

CHAPTER ONE

In the Beginning

But This Only Happens to Other People: Life Before Adoption

For most people, the decision to adopt comes after traditional ways of creating a family are exhausted. In my case, that was partially true. From 1982-1985 I'd undergone the full gamut of infertility treatments in my quest to become pregnant. Adoption came up many times as I was choking down fertility drugs, monitoring my temperature for ovulation predictors and having my entire life taken over by a twenty-eight-day cycle. It was so consuming that I once wrote "Day 17" on the dateline of a check. Now, you're probably thinking that's when we made the decision. Wrong. The treatments eventually worked and on November 19, 1985, I gave birth to a beautiful baby boy.

For the next thirteen years, life fell into a benign pattern—house in the suburbs of Annapolis; my husband was a tenured professor at a local college, and I was fortunate enough to be a working-from-home mom. Kyle was a happy kid, even after he hit the teen years when smiles and chatter were replaced by surly grunts and eye rolls. He had a great sense of humor and used that to charm his way out of almost any situation.

Then in early August 1999, Kyle complained of shortness of breath and chest pains. We did what parents do—we made a doctor's appointment. While the initial diagnosis was asthma, the doctor did refer us to a pediatric cardiology specialist. That appointment was scheduled for five days later. Only we never made it. Two days before his appointment with the specialist, Kyle was rushed to Shock Trauma in Baltimore. My husband and I were thinking this is serious, but our son was thirteen and, until relatively recently, a healthy child. Within twelve hours, a doctor came to us and quietly explained that tests showed Kyle was suffering from cardiomyopathy. I had no idea what that meant, I just knew from the look on the doctor's face that it wasn't good. "So," I asked, "how do we fix it?"

The doctor glanced down at the floor for what felt like a year, then looked up and said, "The options are limited."

My brain couldn't process what that meant. I began peppering the doctor with questions and, as he was answering me, a priest joined us. I vaguely remember wondering why a priest would be roaming the halls of the pediatric intensive care unit at two in the morning. Then I heard the words no parent wants to hear. "Your son's chances of survival are minimal."

Holding my husband's hand like a lifeline and certain I'd misunderstood the doctor, I asked, "Are you telling me Kyle is going to die?"

The doctor nodded. "Without a heart transplant, he has no chance of survival."

In a nanosecond, I said, "Then do it."

Again, the doctor eyed the floor. "It isn't that simple. Only a small percentage of organs become available and the likelihood of finding a match while your son is still a viable transplant recipient . . ."

The long recitation of the inner workings of the organ procurement process didn't make it past my shock and rage.

I thought that conversation and the ones that followed, as we were introduced to the transplant team, the cardiac care team, the social worker, and even an insurance claims representative, signaled the lowest point in my life. I was wrong; my hell was just beginning.

For the next twenty-one days, surrounded by friends and family—with the exception of my parents, who came up from South Carolina and then bailed at the first opportunity—Kyle's condition deteriorated. Massive, successive heart attacks necessitated putting him on an artificial pump to keep him alive until a donor heart could be found. In spite of the valiant efforts of the medical team, a complication developed and a blood clot went to Kyle's brain. On September 2, 1999, we were informed that Kyle was no longer on the transplant list. Tests showed he was brain dead.

Even though he was only breathing because of a respirator, I refused to give up hope. I prayed to God, I cursed God. I begged and pleaded for a miracle. None came. On September 7, 1999, my husband and I stood at our son's bedside as life support was terminated. Within minutes, our beloved son, the one we had struggled so long and hard to conceive, the one I had shared a heartbeat with for nine months, the absolute joy of my life, died in the stark, sparse hospital room.

As we left the building that final time, I kept thinking this had to be some sort of mistake. This kind of tragedy happens to other people, not me. But it wasn't a mistake. And as the months passed, I tried to decide if I was still a mother if I didn't have a child. I needed the loss to make sense. To have meaning. Something, _anything_ to help put the pieces of my shattered life back together. An impossible task. Being a mom was part of my definition of myself. I knew I'd never be whole again if I didn't find some way to move forward.

Six months after Kyle died, my husband and I sat and

talked about our future. Almost simultaneously, we acknowledged that we weren't finished being parents yet. Just as we had done fourteen years earlier during the trials and tribulations of infertility, we discussed adoption. This time, there was no vacillation or hesitation. We were going to build a family; we just had to figure out how to go about it. So we turned—where else?—to the Internet.

Traci Hall

CHAPTER ONE
In the Beginning

But It Has To Be the Flu

I remember being flat on my back on the hospital bed and staring at the pocked ceiling of the Urgent Care Center. I knew I was dying.

I was sure the cramping of my belly was caused by the same flu that was killing kids and elderly in our community at an alarming rate.

Puking is not my thing—wasn't then, and it still isn't. I'd been heaving and praying to the toilet bowl gods forever. Weeks, anyway, and while I wasn't in danger of wasting away, I was so tired that imminent death didn't seem that bad of a deal.

I was eighteen—old enough to know better about lots of things, and young enough to believe that I was invincible. Jaded enough to think that I was untouchable and yet insignificant.

Man, was I busted.

Staring at the ceiling, making deals with whoever was running the universe that this flu I was suffering from wasn't the nine-month kind.

The nurse took my temperature and my blood pressure, while my mom and Loren, my soon-to-be stepdad, stayed at my bedside in the all-white room. The open window allowed morning light to spill in, feigning warmth the January weather didn't contain.

Mom wore a worried expression, her arms crossed. My mom's fiancé looked a little more cautious, but still caring. She'd asked without asking if anything 'else' could be the matter. Like, um, you know…

I had self-righteously shaken my head no. A person had to have sex in order to get pregnant and I, without a boyfriend, was as pure as the…you get the idea.

Nodding her head, my mom championed me and supported my lie all the way to the Urgent Care. The flu going 'round *was* deadly. It was in all of the papers—all over the news.

My story was plausible. And much easier to accept than the alternative—which I'd already pushed from my mind.

But like touching the empty socket of your gum after losing a tooth, I couldn't stop myself from going there.

Dread, worse than anything I'd yet managed to put down on paper—and angst was my specialty—filled the rational part of my brain.

Yeah, that flu was deadly, all right—for anybody under 60 pounds or over a hundred years old. I didn't qualify in either case. But, my God—yes, the same God whom I insisted with my tough-girl snarl didn't exist—*it had just been that one time.*

I couldn't possibly be… *No.*

The nurse was in the room hanging up an IV to replenish my fluids when the doctor came in and asked if there could be the slightest possibility of pregnancy. What could I possibly say with my mom standing right next to me, *supporting* me?

I lied and said, oh no. Definitely not.

Compounding sins, I know, but I wasn't even done.

The day was early yet.

He and the nurse exchanged a knowing look and left the room.

An hour passed. An hour that crawled as slow as a two-legged cockroach, determined to get there, just... compromised.

Like me.

My eighteen-year-old dreams centered around singing and writing lyrics for songs. Writing stories that mattered. Making a difference in the world in the only way I knew how.

That hour held plenty of time to think about all the things I'd screwed up on. It was easy—so easy—to blame my messed up childhood. I'd used that excuse for all sorts of rebellious behavior, but as bad as I thought I could be, I never quite sank to that brick-wall level of tough. I knew I had people who loved me, which made being a *total* bitch kind of difficult.

Even with a mohawk, I tended to be more of a Pollyanna than a Charles Manson.

I don't know if times were different then, or if it was just being raised at the poverty level by a single mom, but going to college wasn't ever an expectation.

Whenever my uncle was in town, we'd sit on the front porch gabbing over what the future could hold. Possibilities...dreams, nothing solid.

I spent hours and hours drinking coffee and smoking cigarettes at Denny's or Europa, a favorite hangout for other black-clad teens. My friends and I were searching for answers that always seemed just out of reach.

The truth was an elusive ghost that danced on the edge of our lives, and we wanted to hold it. We talked about success, we talked about moving, we *talked* until our jaws were sore. Not once do I recall saying, "Hey, I wanna be knocked up from a one-night stand and be a struggling, single mom on welfare." I don't remember any of my friends saying that either.

I worked. Didn't matter what color my hair was, I always had a job that paid for my coffee, smokes, and fast food. My mom had bills to pay and she was a few months away from getting married. I'd turned eighteen and wasn't her responsibility anymore—not that she ever, ever said that.

At the time, I got around by bus pass. Spokane has the best bus system of anyplace I've ever lived. Curfew was 1:00 a.m. and the last bus ran at 12:45. It was also cheap.

It was sometimes dangerous downtown, but I carried my attitude like armor—an outwardly tough chick with more bravado than a good solid left punch.

I mostly hung with the punk crowd, on the fringes of everything. My one and only fight was downtown in Riverfront Park, where I got my ass handed to me on a platter by the rockers. One girl in particular didn't like her boyfriend talking to me down on Riverside.

These were situations that I put myself in because I thought I had something to prove. I was alive, but what did I have for life experiences other than the crap I'd had no control over?

High school was over and I didn't want to work at Newberry's forever, so I'd decided to go to business school.

I loved color; I loved edgy fashion. For five thousand bucks, I could have a degree in Fashion Merchandising. I could live in Seattle with the other trendsetters and forward thinkers.

In the Beginning

Ah…escape from the blah-ness of Spokane, Washington. Mountains and brown plains surrounded a sprawling city of gray industry. Everybody I knew under the age of twenty-five wanted out.

It was the mid-eighties and bands like Vampire Lesbos and Diddly Squat raged in empty warehouses or rented studio space. Pre-grunge garage sounds kicked butt. The cover charge to see the band was never more than five bucks, and if you didn't have the cash, somebody would sneak you in, in exchange for a beer.

We were searching for something 'more' in loud punk music, violence and alcohol.

And yeah, sex. Despite the Aids epidemic, we took chances that we shouldn't have—although chlamydia was more prevalent than pregnancy. 'Friends' could make group appointments down at the clinic. You always knew who was sleeping with whom by who was taking the same meds.

It was almost a joke, only not very funny.

There wasn't a pill or a cream for what was making me sick. And when the doctor came back into the room, an uncomfortable look on his face, and announced that I was pregnant?

My belly cramped up big time, and the cool fluid from the IV flowed into my veins like slush.

In that one instant, I knew my life was forever changed. I couldn't hide this problem, I couldn't put a band-aid over it, and I couldn't ignore it.

I was going to have a baby.

I didn't even like kids.

I was still a kid! I wasn't done growing up.

My mom's face was pale and Loren's eyebrows went up,

but neither one of them said a word. The doctor left as if his little white coat were on fire.

Oh my God...

This kind of situation didn't happen on the Cosby show, and I couldn't think of one good thing to come from it.

The father of this baby wasn't going to be very happy either. I hardly knew him!

Pregnant?

Now what?

All of these thoughts snapped through my mind like lightning across a dark, stormy sky.

Shame and shock were at the front of the line for emotional overload.

"Well?" my mom asked into the oncoming storm.

With my back against the wall, I pulled out my attitude and announced, "I'm having an abortion!" Then I burst into tears.

Rhonda Pollero

Now What?

Turning Despair into Decision: Adoption Options and Angst

You'd think the State—any State—would be thrilled to get a call from prospective parents wanting to adopt an older child. After discussing the issue, my husband and I decided that we had only two criteria for finding our child: we wanted a girl and we didn't want an infant. The vast majority of prospective parents want a baby—not us. So imagine my shock when I contacted Social Services and a very bored-sounding counselor explained to me that in order to adopt out of the foster care system, my husband and I would need to be foster parents for a minimum of seven years. Um, what?

I was forty, my husband was sixty. We were financially stable and had been married for nearly twenty years. We even watched the "Wednesday's Child" segment on the news every week and listened to the interviewer pleading for families to adopt these children. We knew there were children who needed homes and we were ready, willing and able to welcome a child into our home. Learning disabilities weren't a huge obstacle. My husband was a career educator, I was a writer, and we had the luxury of knowing we could devote the time and energy to a special needs child. Was this woman serious?

Yep. Though she did mention an exception. I was thrilled. For about ten seconds. The exception was if we were willing to take a child with AIDS or some other terminal illness. Call me a selfish, horrible person, but I couldn't do it. I didn't have the fortitude to sit by and watch another child die.

On to Plan B: international adoption. When we shared our decision with others, the naysayers came out of the woodwork. For good reason. International adoption has its own inherent problems. We knew a couple who'd adopted from South America. The five-year-old they'd adopted turned out to be a malnourished eleven-year-old with several sexually transmitted diseases and a severe attachment disorder. Another couple had adopted from Eastern Europe and their son had emotional and behavioral problems that required removal from the home for in-patient, residential treatment.

The plus to international adoption is that the chances of a birth mother or father knocking on your door months or years after the adoption are almost nil. The downside is the maze of paperwork and corruption you've got to navigate to make it happen.

Then there were the general pessimists. Those people who seemed to take great pleasure in telling us that we'd end up with a severely damaged child because they'd seen segments on television and were self-proclaimed experts on the pitfalls of international adoption.

Then came the category threes—those people who praised us for replacing Kyle. Are you kidding me? Ask any parent with more than one child if they see them as interchangeable. Note to the cat threes: by that logic, I should have at least two husbands in case something happens to hubby number one.

Now What?

I also kept wondering why a great many people thought an adopted child should come with a lifetime warranty, yet the same standard doesn't seem to apply to biological children. They aren't Fords™, they're children. Between us, my husband and I have thirteen years of college, so it wasn't as if we were making an uninformed or rash decision. I'm using the term 'we' rather loosely. Like most things, my husband developed a case of 'man syndrome' during a lot of the investigative process. Translation: I did the legwork and gave him a report of my findings. Adoption Cliff's Notes, if you will.

It wasn't lack of interest on his part, just the rearing-of-the-husband habit of letting-the-spouse-do-most-of-the-work beast. Men are really good at employing this tact. This is especially true when it comes to all things children. Ever notice how when men are watching their own children it's referred to as babysitting? All they have to do is take their kid to the park or a movie one time and they are practically nominated for sainthood for being such 'involved' fathers. Men are asked if they change diapers and if they answer in the affirmative, they are applauded. When was the last time you heard someone ask a mom *if* she changes diapers? I'd love to see Gloria Allred take this one on.

I digress. Back to the decision to adopt. For whatever reason, my husband wasn't on the receiving end of a lot of the negative comments. Just like with the babysitting thing, he was basically applauded for making the world a better place by welcoming another child into his life. I should mention that he has two children from a previous marriage. At the time we were considering adoption, his kids were both over thirty. So my husband got bonus kudos for deciding to have another child when most of his contemporaries were well beyond their child-rearing stage.

Me? I got blow-by-blow recitations of the horror stories

featured on news magazine shows. It's the adoption equivalent of being pregnant and having virtual strangers share their pregnancy/birth horror stories when you're a month away from your due date. Thanks, as if it wasn't a hard enough decision without hearing about someone's cousin's neighbor's sister's adoption that fell through at the court hearing in Guatemala after said cousin's neighbor's sister had spent nearly thirty thousand dollars just to come back to the US with empty arms.

We got mixed reactions from our respective families, running the gamut from unconditional support to outright disapproval. My husband has three brothers, all of whom are childless by choice. One thought we were plain nuts to even consider adoption. The other two were cautiously supportive. My stepchildren were unwavering in their support. They understood that our decision to adopt wasn't about Kyle's death, rather our need to go on living. More than a decade earlier, my sister and her husband had welcomed two children into their home. At the time, the kids were twelve and thirteen. My sister and her family were also completely supportive.

I honestly don't know what my parents thought during that time. We aren't a bare-your-soul kind of family. Every substantive issue was swept under the rug or met with that dreaded brick wall of parental silence. I did have reason to be concerned, though. Neither my stepchildren nor my sister's adopted children had ever been truly embraced by my parents, so I wasn't sure what to expect. I did know that if they disapproved, it wouldn't be the first time, and I was okay with that possibility. Our close friends were universally supportive, even those who'd suffered adoption horror stories of their own.

Once we had a plan, it was time for more research. I'm the kind of dork who reads the manuals for the television, so doing the legwork was definitely within my comfort zone. Some countries I excluded right off the bat. Some had residency rules stipulating prospective adoptive parents had to live in the country from three to nine months prior to filing for adoption. That wasn't viable. I was the one with the mobile job—I could write anyplace—but I had no desire to live apart from my husband for close to a year.

After reading an article about orphaned girls in China, I told my husband I thought that might be the best choice for us. Female children are not valued in China and since we wanted a girl and didn't feel it was important that the child physically resemble us, China sounded perfect.

The second part of Plan B was to find an agency that specialized in international adoptions. From my research, I'd learned that one of the keys to a successful adoption experience was working with an agency that knew the rules and regulations of the countries and had a good track record dealing with INS. (Note: INS has since been placed under the umbrella of Homeland Security, but more on that later.) There were two agencies in the Baltimore-Washington-Annapolis triangle with impeccable reputations. For the sake of convenience, I chose the one closest to my home.

Unlike my call to Social Services a month earlier, I was greeted by an enthusiastic, supportive, informative woman who was an adoptive mother herself. She made time in her schedule to meet with me the following day. I was thrilled, to say the least.

We met and I adored her on sight. She was organized, positive, and in less than twenty-four hours had already put together a file with prospective children she thought would meet our criteria. Tit-for-tat, I was going to impress her with my own research. I proudly pulled out my file and placed it on the polished mahogany conference table. Eagerly, I announced that my husband and I had decided on China, but before I could finish the first sentence on why I thought China was the perfect country, she politely interrupted me.

"I'm sorry, but you and your husband aren't eligible to adopt from China."

I was stunned. Was it that we were Catholic? Hey, I'd happily put a statue of Buddha in our potential daughter's bedroom. Hell, I'd hang a poster of Moa Tse-tung in her room if that's what the Chinese government required. Rumor had it that baby girls were held in such low esteem in China that they were drowned to make room for male children in the State-run orphanages. I was flexible; I'd happily incorporate anything necessary to give a little girl a home. Plus, my sister's children were Korean-American, so in my mind, I was doubly qualified to welcome a child of Asian descent into my home. "How," I asked, "could we not be eligible? We're freaking perfect!"

She smiled patiently and said, "Combined age."

I didn't know what that meant, but it didn't sound promising. There was a math component to adoption? Immediately I began to sweat, harkening back to that seventh grade algebra word problem… If a train leaves L.A. at noon travelling sixty mph and another train leaves NYC at midnight travelling ninety mph, how many brunettes get off the L.A. train in Detroit?

Obviously, this wasn't going to be as easy as I thought.

Traci Hall

CHAPTER TWO
Now What?

Okay, So I Had Sex
Abortion, Adoption and Indecision

I sat outside and smoked in the chilled air while my mom took care of the paperwork. My head was spinning and my body was reeling with so much—emotion, hormones, excuses, fear.

Happiness was noticeably absent. I'd messed around and gotten caught, and now I had to pay the price. Happy was not on my radar.

Leaning forward, I wiped hot tears from my face, but they fell so fast I couldn't keep up, and I finally just let them fall. I knew I would never be *happy* again.

Abortion would be the easiest way out. Nobody would ever have to know that I'd been so stupid.

Who gets pregnant? It had been a one-night stand— unplanned. *Dumb, dumb, dumb.* What would I tell Ricky? My stomach burned with regret and bile.

My mom came out, my almost stepdad right behind her. As usual, Loren was a pillar of calm in a sea of chaos.

"I'm not having this baby," I announced again, wanting to fight—with anybody.

He nodded. My mom didn't say anything. What could

she say? I wasn't dying of the flu after all—and my news reflected on her, too.

I'd lied, and not just about the sex thing.

I'm sure she had questions. Like who the daddy was...and when had I managed to sleep around? I lived at home and didn't have a boyfriend.

Shame heated my skin from the inside out, and I knew I was flushed, which made me cling to the false bravery behind my attitude. Still nauseous, I put my smoke out and we walked to the car without speaking.

I had some explaining to do, but I didn't have the answers.

Ricky, a seventeen-year-old Seattle punk, who was sofa surfing at my friend's house while I'd visited during a Fashion Merchandising field trip, was the father.

We'd exchanged phone calls and letters before we'd ever met face to face, so it wasn't like he'd been a total stranger, but still, we weren't exactly in a monogamous, committed relationship.

I had to call him—or not—depending on what I was going to do.

My inner mantra on the way home went a little like this: *I'm going to have an abortion, and my life will go back to normal. I'm going to have an abortion, and my life will go back to normal. I'm going to have an abortion, and my life will go back to normal.*

If I said it enough, maybe I'd start to believe it. My outer, tough chick was ready to box us out of the proverbial corner. But...

The God I swore I didn't believe in was calling my bluff.

But...

Now What?

An abortion would let me pretend this never happened.

I couldn't have a baby! I didn't like babies or diapers or responsibility. I imagined a life on welfare as a single mom—*trapped* forever in Spokane. I envisioned myself hunched over a typewriter, as I worked on my creative masterpiece, while the baby slept or cried or *needed* me.

My friends would all move on—leave the State, or at least hitchhike across the mountains. I'd be tethered to a dingy apartment with a screaming infant.

If I had an abortion, I wouldn't have to suffer the humiliation of admitting to the world I'd been stupid. An abortion would let me sweep my mistake under the carpet, and the only person I'd have to apologize to would be myself.

Abortion.

I convinced myself that I was really, honestly going to do it.

By the time we got home, I had my mind made up. My armor was firmly in place, and I was ready to take on the world.

Sure, my mom might be ashamed of my decision, but it wouldn't be for long. She'd get over it.

We could forget this ever happened and go on with our lives, uninterrupted. Hey, Ricky wouldn't even have to know. I was feeling like a saint, as I thought of all of the pain I was saving him from by keeping my pregnancy and abortion a secret.

My belly was a pit of boiling lava. My face was raw from crying, and my head pounded with each step I took to my room.

I didn't want to talk—I wanted to die. And I needed to be alone to sort it all out.

Now What?

Alone, in teen speak, meant that I needed my friends. I got a hold of Michelle and Carrie, but Robbie was out. Carrie, who had regular access to a car, picked us all up and we took our favorite back booth at Denny's, huddled over coffee and cigarettes.

Now that I knew I was pregnant, I felt guilty lighting up. I reminded my nagging conscious that it didn't matter if I smoked. I was going to have an abortion. This was back at a time when you could still smoke in McDonalds, and the high school had a smoker's corner.

The anti-smoking campaign hadn't hit its stride yet. *And really, Ma, everybody does it…*

Defiant, I puffed away while we sat and dissected the facts, which went like this:

Carrie: Oh my God, pregnant? You don't even know this guy! He lives in Seattle. What are you going to do?

Michelle: Oh. My. God. Pregnant…this sucks. Are you going to tell Ricky? He's going to want to know.

Me: Oh my God! I'm *pregnant*! I don't know if I should tell Ricky or not, I mean, we're still talking on the phone a few times a week, but he lives in Seattle.

Carrie: You can get an abortion. He can pay for half.

Michelle: Abortion? I don't know.

Me: I'm getting an abortion! I've already decided. How much do they cost?

Carrie: Dunno. The sooner the better, right?

Michelle: I heard you can get one up to five months pregnant.

Me: That's gross. That's a baby.

Carrie: Technically, so is this (she gestures at the general vicinity of my belly with her hand, and the smoke follows like a trail).

Michelle: What if Ricky wants to keep it?

Carrie: Who cares what he wants?

Me: I *don't* care. (lie, lie) My body, my choice. I don't think I'll tell him.

Michelle: You *have* to tell him. He has a right to know.

Carrie: (snorting) He doesn't have any rights.

Me: (crying) I can't *believe* I'm pregnant. (Stomach gurgling, bile rising, hot and sour up the back of my throat) I gotta go.

The scene ends with me in the bathroom, hurling coffee until my back aches.

We had so many conversations that went just like that. Struggling with my Catholic School conscious was exhausting, and after a few days, I decided that Michelle was right. I had to call Ricky.

Sofa surfing doesn't allow for a personal phone number, and this was when cell phones were the size of a shoe box and cost about a thousand dollars.

They weren't for everybody.

Our system was that I'd call whatever number Ricky thought he might be at, hoping that he wasn't in downtown Seattle at a club or rave. Or if he was at the place he'd arranged to be at, that he wasn't already too trashed to talk.

Ricky wasn't exactly my boyfriend, but we were more than friends, and since we'd met (slept together) we'd gotten to know each other a lot better by phone and letters. There was no such thing as email—I feel like I'm writing about the dark ages.

I had to trust that our budding relationship would weather this latest storm. I thought he would be very much on board with my getting an abortion and moving on with life.

I was wrong.

Maybe he reacted to how I told him I was pregnant. I guess I dropped the news with all of the finesse of a bomb going off on an elementary school playground. He freaked out, and I, regretfully, admit that I felt in control—until the next wave of nausea kicked me back to the curb.

He was unprepared, and so was I.

I thought I needed to do the right thing for us… him…me. But was it the right thing…or just the easiest thing?

Maybe Ricky heard the underlying doubt in my voice during our long, late-night conversations. He was supportive of whatever I wanted, albeit reluctantly.

I was surprised that he was having such a hard time with this. He didn't practice his childhood religion any more than I did, but it seems we each wrestled with the morality of abortion, in part due to our upbringing.

Ricky had been raised Jehovah's Witness, and I was Catholic.

This brought our relationship into question. I didn't mind having a sort of boyfriend in Seattle. It left me free to do whatever I wanted in Spokane, which was go to school so that I could get a cool job. It gave me someone to visit and hang with in Seattle, providing I didn't mind where we crashed.

He asked me to wait a few more days before I did anything, so that he could catch a Greyhound over the mountains and come to me like a punk rock Sir Galahad.

How could I say no?

Ricky was being incredibly sweet—and very naïve. Even though I knew that, it gave me the excuse I was looking for to not make an immediate appointment at Planned Parenthood.

Something I'd been dragging my feet about.

Planned Parenthood was for picking up free birth control pills, and I'd already missed that boat. I didn't have insurance, so what were they going to do? Hand me a scrawled list of back-alley doctor's names? Physicians who would secretly rid me of my problem...for a fee and a pint of Jack Daniels?

I didn't really know what to expect, and the curse of an active imagination is that my mind veered toward the worst possible scenario.

I'd gone with friends while they waited at the clinic to pick up medicine, and I hated the beige walls and the brown plaid furniture. It had a certain desperate smell, something in between stale smoke and diapers. The threadbare nap carpet had stains on it, and broken toys littered the tiny kid's table.

Posters advised abstinence, which was ironic, considering the name of the place. By the time anybody needed Planned Parenthood, they were pretty much doing the wild thing.

I had no clue what to do. Apathy was easier than making a decision, and waiting for Ricky was an excellent reason to do nothing.

Instead, I spent all my time puking, or thinking about puking or sucking saltines so that I wouldn't puke. Cigarettes started to make me seriously ill, and I couldn't stand eggs.

I craved Nalley's chili from a can, and cried if there

wasn't any in the house. The only thing that calmed my belly for up to an hour was mashed potatoes and gravy from Kentucky Fried Chicken.

I spent more time with my head in the toilet than anywhere else. Everybody told me that the morning sickness wouldn't last more than three months.

Liars! I was at the least faintly nauseous all through my pregnancy. Three months...ha. And who came up with the title of morning sickness? That stuff lasted all day.

We had to tell close family and friends about my condition, just to explain my suddenly bolting for the nearest bathroom. After the initial shock wore off, nobody knew what to say to me. What could they say?

Hallmark doesn't make an Abortion card.

My friends, while supportive, didn't really know how to make things better. I was in limbo and dragging them with me.

I couldn't drink coffee, I couldn't smoke, I couldn't go to parties, and I was tired of talking about it. I cried or yelled or gagged as I railed against fate.

Not exactly easy to be around...

Ricky tried to come to Spokane, but he just couldn't. He didn't have a job, which meant that he never had money. He didn't want his parents to know—they didn't even know about me. Ricky had moved out because his parents didn't understand him. It was a popular teen sentiment, but not cool when you needed help and couldn't get it.

I was over two months pregnant, and I had to make a decision that wasn't based on anybody's feelings but my own. Ricky meant well, and I know that he cared about me, but he was no more prepared to be a daddy than I was to be a mom.

Now What?

I knew that the longer I stayed pregnant, the harder it would be to…I made myself say it, even though it was getting harder and harder…*kill the baby.*

Just thinking about it made me sick down to my very soul.

I believe it is a woman's right to choose. I am one hundred percent Pro Choice, and I will defend anybody's right to have an abortion if they feel they need to.

In my opinion, it shouldn't be used as birth control, but things happen that are overwhelming, and it should be an option.

With real, sober doctors and no coat hangers.

I think I was very afraid of what it would be like, knowing that I'd been responsible for extinguishing the spark of life inside me. Could I live with that? I didn't know.

I was starting to realize that the answer was no. It would make my life too hard. I wanted the easiest way out, but I had to live with myself, too. But I couldn't be a mom!

What was I supposed to do?

Some days I was so sick that I wondered if I would even carry the baby to term. I made deals with myself… that if I didn't miscarry by such and such a date, THEN I would call the abortion clinic.

Two weeks passed. I continued to work at Newberry's, I went to class, and I kept my secret. I did research, read pamphlets, and searched my heart. By the third month, I knew I couldn't have the abortion.

The guilt would kill me.

It dawned on me that not having an abortion meant that I was going to have a baby. A real, live human being growing to the size of a football would be inside of my stomach.

A new kind of terror gripped me as I tried to grasp what the future might hold. It was too big and overwhelming.

Telling myself I'd have an abortion had allowed me to think about things in the short term. Three months, and my life would be back on track.

Now I had another six plus months of pregnancy to look forward to. I didn't have insurance, which was going to be a problem. I was going to have to tell people I'd gotten pregnant and that my boyfriend lived in Seattle. I counted ahead and realized that I couldn't stay in Fashion Merchandising and graduate before the baby would be born.

What job could I really get with a degree in fashion merchandising, anyway? I wasn't tall or exotically beautiful. I didn't have a knack for putting chic and timeless outfits together. My style tended toward eclectic.

Besides, I'd tried working at a few clothing stores and absolutely despised it.

Being pregnant made my nose extra sensitive (that and not smoking), and the perfumes and scents of Mariposa made my toes curl. The salesgirls all acted like they should have been walking a catwalk somewhere, and were only stocking skirts and belts until they were 'discovered.'

What I'd thought would be an easy ticket out of Spokane and into the edgy Seattle scene didn't appeal to me at all.

So, I confessed my problem to my Fashion Merchandising teacher, and she helped me transfer into Floral Design and Business Management.

I assured her it wasn't her fault that I'd met Ricky and gotten pregnant while on her field trip, but I know she felt awful about it. She checked in on me all through my classes and encouraged me to finish. She was a great teacher.

Now What?

If everything went as planned, I would graduate right around the time my baby was due. I needed a goal to set my sights on, and this seemed like a doable one. Besides, it kept my mind off the baby and what to do after...

While a part of me was relieved that I'd made the decision not to have an abortion, the rest of me was now afraid of what was coming up.

Could I handle having a baby? Nurture a little life until that person grew to adulthood? The idea scared me to death.

Making a list of things I'd need to get done, I thought about a place to live.

Panicked, I figured that my mom and Loren would let me live with them. They knew me—they knew I couldn't be relied on to wake up when the baby cried!

Or what if I forgot the baby on the bus? I didn't have a car. Who would watch him during the day? Would I work? What could I do that would get me insurance and dental?

I sucked as a human being—how on earth was I supposed to learn how to be a mom?

It should have been impossible to feel like a bigger loser, and yet I managed.

My mom—thank God for my mom—suggested adoption. I told her she was crazy, but she made an appointment to 'just listen' about possible adoption programs.

This wasn't my ideal choice (that should have been abstinence four months prior), but it made me feel less trapped.

In my mind, always prominent was an image of me working and slaving for twenty years, with a thousand squealing babies at my feet. I weighed five hundred pounds, chain-smoked and wore a bad floral print apron as I made gruel to feed my poor, poor children.

I agreed to go. Just to listen.

We walked in. I remember feeling very reserved about the whole thing. I was terrified, the kind of scared one has of the unknown. I was relieved that I hadn't gone through with an abortion, but I could barely wrap my mind around a nine-month-long guest.

Doubt about raising a child kept me mired in uncertainty, but I wasn't sure that I could go through with giving my baby to strangers.

What if they were bad parents?

What if they ended up getting divorced, or having a secret gambling addiction? What if this child grew up lonely and confused, never knowing his own history?

And, even worse, curse my imagination, what if someday I had other kids and they dated their sibling?

Stranger things have been known to happen.

My mom sat next to me as the lady went on and on about adoption being 'the only choice that mattered.' She assured me that the State put parents through a rigorous background check, and that the records were sealed until the child turned eighteen. Then, if I signed the right paperwork, that child could locate me. If I wanted to remain anonymous, then I would sign a different paper that would then be filed in the courthouse.

I hated the idea of not knowing where my child might go, but the lady coldly stated that this was the way adoption was done.

After ten minutes of this, she asked my mom and me to sit down in another room while she showed us a little film.

I was thinking we'd be watching happy families receiving cute babies wrapped in pink or blue blankets.

The reality of the aborted baby parts was enough to make me sick.

And furious. I stood up and asked her what she was thinking—we were there to discuss adoption, not abortion.

Her answer, that this was a standard part of their interview process, made me even more furious. My mom totally understood, and we left before we throttled her. If she was expecting gratitude for that show, she had another thing coming.

I was so angry that I was shaking all the way to the car. By choosing to hear about adoption, I was pretty much stating my choice to not have an abortion. We had no need to watch that display. My mom and I both felt that the State's idea of pro-adoption left a lot to be desired.

We never went back, and my view of adoption was soured.

Now what?

Abortion—no.

Adoption—no.

I only had one option left. I was going to end up a single parent on welfare—something that really went against my grain. But when I got home, Ricky called. And proposed.

Rhonda Pollero

CHAPTER THREE

The Good, The Bad and the Ugly

I Have to Do What and Go Where?

The Exciting But Sometimes Daunting Process of International Adoption

Or, How I Learned to Hate the Word "Apositiled"

Turns out, combined age is exactly what it sounds like. It's a simple calculation of adding your ages together to come up with a combined age. In our case, we were one hundred years old. That magic, albeit arbitrary, number has more power than kryptonite. That number has the ability to exclude a couple from eligibility to adopt from many countries.

For us, it meant good-bye China. The maximum combined age in 2000 was 94. Our combined age limited us to two countries—Russia and Romania. Well, three if you count the fact that Estonia was about to open up to foreign adoption, so if we wanted to wait some indeterminate period of time, there might have been a third option.

We had friends who'd adopted from Russia, so Russia it was. Silly me, I thought selecting a country was going to be the difficult part. I couldn't have been more wrong. Each country has its own set of requirements. Translation: redundant paperwork that makes the IRS look like slackers. While the adoption agent had a child in mind whom she thought would be perfect for us, we had to complete round one of the paperwork before she'd even tell us the age of the little girl.

By that afternoon, my dining room table had been transformed into Adoption Central. Pretty much what you'd expect—birth certificates, marriage certificates, three years worth of tax returns, employment verification, deeds, financial statements, etc. All pretty straightforward stuff. Except for one minor detail. Certified copies don't cut it. You have to get a certified copy of each document, then take it to the Secretary of State and have it apositiled. In case you didn't know, apositiled is the process of getting certified documents stamped at a cost(in 2000) of $5.00 per page. We had thirty-five pages to be apositiled. Ka-ching. Not to mention that this process entails a person sitting behind a reception desk with a roll of gold seal stickers. After collecting your cash (no checks accepted), smacking a sticker on the page, and then sending you on your way. I never met the Secretary of State—never even so much as had a sighting—but I guess that didn't matter. So long as the person behind the desk had an opposable thumb, I was golden.

With my apositiled documents in my hand, I'm thinking I'm home free. The only other task is to be fingerprinted by the State and the FBI. Piece of cake, right? Wrong. The FBI was easy; they have an optical scanning system that is pretty much idiot-proof. My local police station had an elderly volunteer auxiliary officer. My husband and I traipse in, do the ink and roll and think, that was pretty easy. Then a week later, we're notified that my husband's prints were too smeared and voided by the consulate. So he goes back and gets reprinted.

The Good, the Bad, and the Ugly

A week after that, I get my do-over card. A week after that, my husband gets notification number two. Ditto a week later for me. One whole month was devoted to fingerprinting. My patience was running thin and, just as an aside, fingerprint ink is hell on a manicure. Finally, we had all the documents and were ready to go back to the agency and formally file our request to adopt from Russia and *finally* get some information on our little girl in Russia.

The first thing I noticed was yet another pile of papers in the center of the mahogany table. My hopes that they might be waiting for some other family were dashed the minute I saw the sticky note with 'Pollero' scrawled in black marker. I groaned audibly, wondering what additional information could be required. My kindergarten attendance records? My SAT scores? My BMI? Lord knew I'd already provided everything, including a physician's certification of physical fitness.

Deflated, I took a seat as soon as our agency representative entered the room. She must have sensed my enthusiasm waning, because she was quick to point out that the tower of forms in the center of the table was nothing more than immigration and VISA applications, oh, and a list of immunizations we'd need in order to travel to Kursk.

Kursk? My ears perked up. I had no idea where Kursk was and I didn't care. I finally had something tangible—my daughter lived in Kursk. Even though it only took a couple of seconds, it felt like days before she slowly slipped a 2 x 3 photograph of a little girl from the folder she kept clutched to her chest.

I looked at the face of an angel and instantly started to cry. I was holding the adoption equivalent of a sonogram and emotion overwhelmed us both. My husband's eyes welled with tears, turning my cries into body-wrenching sobs.

The Good, the Bad, and the Ugly

We began firing off questions. "How old is she?"

"Three."

"What's her name?"

"They call her Tashya, but the birth certificate we have lists a different name."

"What?"

Our agent sat down and explained the Russian orphanage system to us, then proceeded to give us a history on our daughter. She was very sure about the Russian system but, apparently, this child's brief life history was, like most Russian Orphans, part fact, part fiction, and part conjecture. Because the original was written in Cyrillic and the translation was provided by the orphanage, she warned us that the information may not be true and accurate. I didn't really care. I was looking at a beautiful little girl with sad, lonely green eyes in a tattered blue dress seated in a dreary room. I wanted to leave for Russia on the next flight.

Enter stack of paperwork number two. The good news was it seemed we only had a few more things to get done to complete our file. A social worker had to do a home study and a few unannounced visits. We had to prepare a room for our daughter and have the fire marshal check our home for any safety violations. That sounded doable, and I hadn't heard the dreaded "apositiled" word in conjunction with any of the round two requirements.

We had to apply to the Russian government for VISAs, a simple process we were told. Complete one form, enclose a check, and just make sure we request the multiple-visit option. My head whipped up. Multiple visits? She explained that in rare instances, the Russian court system requires several trips but she didn't think that would be the case. The extended VISA was just precautionary. I relaxed.

The Good, the Bad, and the Ugly

I also wrote a check to the agency that day, a pretty hefty one. Apparently, because of our combined age, we'd be paying a premium in fees. Oh well, I looked at those sad green eyes again and didn't flinch at the twenty-plus thousand dollar check.

The final requirement was gifts to our host country.

We were handed a neatly typed, two-page list of 'gifts' we needed to take when we went to Russia. I understood the baby vitamins and the formula and the diapers and the shoes and clothes. Then I read on to find vodka, cigarettes, red lipstick, tampons, and a bunch of other items I couldn't fathom being necessities for an orphanage. Well, that's because they weren't for the orphanage, they were for various Russian officials and other 'persons of influence' we'd be dependent upon when in Russia.

I soon learned a 'person of influence' is a euphemism for Russian Mafia. Apparently, nothing gets done in Russia and, more specifically, Kursk without an appropriate offertory to the local mob boss. Again, looking at those green eyes in the photograph dissolved my sense of outrage.

Oh, and one last thing, we needed to be ready to travel at any moment once our VISAs were issued. Russian officials would contact our agency and, in turn, they would tell us when to fly to Moscow. Normally it's a week after the call, so we needed to be prepared to pay $800-$2,000 per ticket. Ka-ching. Oh yeah, they couldn't guarantee that the little girl in the photo will still be at the orphanage when we arrived in Kursk.

My head was spinning. If I understood all this, I was spending thousands of dollars, plus bribes, er, gifts to my host country, in order to adopt a child who might not be there when I arrived after I'd jumped through these last hoops. Didn't exactly sound like an ideal plan, but it was what it was. I was in their sandbox, so I had to play by their rules.

We filled out the VISA forms, wrote yet another check, and sent in our applications. I went out and bought a lifetime supply of tampons, dozens of tubes of red lipstick, and enough kid's shoes and clothing to open my own store. Oh, and I made a special trip to the liquor store for the Sky™ vodka and yes, it did seem weird to be buying vodka to take to Russia. But hey, I was dotting every 'I' and crossing every 'T' just to be on the safe side.

The social worker did the home study, and I think she did all three surprise visits in less than two weeks. We decorated the bedroom and had the fire marshal come over. He promptly cited us for not having a handrail on both sides of the stairs and for having our fire extinguisher in the hall closet and not in the kitchen. Easy fixes, though I had a tiny kitchen, so the roasting pan and the cookie sheets ended up in the hall closet to accommodate the hulking fire extinguisher.

The end was near. I could sense it. I was excited. I was ready. My application for a VISA was rejected. Yep, according to the United States government, I failed to name the state in which I was born; therefore, citizenship could not be verified. Well, I failed to name a state because I was born in Washington, D.C., which, aside from not being a state but rather the nation's capital, was where the office was located that rejected my application. I'm sure it would have been troubling news to the DAR to learn that a clerk did not consider me a citizen.

Thinking, erroneously, of course, that this was just some silly clerical error, I called the INS. I was curtly and promptly told that if I could not provide the name of the state in which I was born, they could not verify my citizenship. Just as curtly, I asked the woman what international border she crossed going to work that morning. Note to those considering foreign adoption: sarcasm does not work on federal government employees.

I grabbed the phone book, called my U.S. senator's office, and explained my dilemma. The senator's aide insisted that I must be mistaken and suggested I resubmit the application. I did. I got rejected again. This whole time I was haunted by the little girl with the sad eyes and my secret fear that if and when I finally made it to Kursk, she'd be gone. So I did the only logical thing. I played the girl card. I called my other U.S. senator's office and, through my tears, explained the problem I was having and added an anguished plea for help. My VISA application was approved the next day.

We did it. All our ducks were in a row. I faxed everything to the adoption agency and half expected our agent to tell me to pack to leave the next day. Well, that didn't happen. It took another four weeks before we received our notification that we needed to be in Russia on the 28th of June. I immediately called the airline, only to discover that most flights were booked. The best I could do was flying out of Virginia, changing planes in Switzerland and landing in Moscow twenty-six hours later. Oh, and only first class was available. Did I want the tickets? Hell yes.

Though the flight was draining, we were both so excited, we barely slept, and when we stepped off the plane, I felt a little like Dorothy landing in Oz, only nothing had been cleaned for a few decades. Everything was covered in a layer of grime, but that wasn't what bothered me most. No, it was knowing that I was technically breaking the law by having more than ten thousand U.S. dollars in my possession as I entered the country. As we worked our way through customs, I half expected one of the pencil-necked soldiers mulling about to arrest me and send me to the nearest gulag.

Instead, the customs inspectors just stole our granola

bars and some of the gifts, and then let us pass. Like cattle going off to slaughter, we were shoved and jostled toward what we hoped was the exit—all the signage was in Cyrillic, so we were pretty much on our own. Eventually, we saw a small man standing on the other side of the chain-link fence holding a sign that read 'Pollermo.' Close enough. In a matter of seconds, we were on him like white on rice. He introduced himself as Alex and explained that he would be our host in Kursk and that we'd be staying at the home he shared with his mother.

After leaving the airport, we were whisked via cab through the congested streets of Moscow. The frenetic pace of the city rivaled New York City, though it was obvious that much of the city was in dire need of repair and restoration. My guess was that it had been some time since anyone had pressure washed any of the public buildings or swept the streets. It quickly became apparent that there are two Moscows: the sanitized, capitalism-embracing version we see on television in the United States and the real Moscow, the one with abject poverty blanketed by layers of dirt and corruption.

Still, for a child of the Cold War, it was fascinating to see Red Square, the Kremlin and the Pushkin Museum. You can't travel more than a few blocks without seeing some sort of monument to fallen World War II heroes. Sadly, with the demise of socialism, no one seemed to be in charge of maintaining the monuments and cemeteries. Weeds and tall grasses all but obliterated parks, and street vendors occupied the city, selling everything from religious icons to knock-off Hard Rock Cafe™ T-shirts. Pirated DVDs are a hot commodity, surpassed only by Levi's™.

The cab delivered us to the train station. Lugging our suitcases, we made our way through the terminal and boarded the train for the 8-10 hour ride south to Kursk.

It was at the train station that I was introduced to a public bathroom, Russian style. Okay, I admit it. I'm a pretty high-maintenance woman with some definite germophobe leanings. I'd rather stick a pencil in my eye than use a Port-a-Potty, but one look at the ladies room had me wishing for one of those outdoor communal potties.

Instead, I faced a gruff-looking woman holding a roll of rough, brown paper. Apparently, one three-by-three square was four rubles. Reaching into my pocket, I counted out 40 rubles for ten squares. She scoffed at me, muttered something in Russian, then snatched forty rubles out of my hand and gave me a single sheet. Even through the language barrier, I got it–one to a customer.

Resigned, I decided to practice my Russian. Well, technically I didn't know any Russian; I'd just learned a few phrases phonetically. Basic stuff like, "Thank you for your assistance," and "It was nice to meet you." Smiling, I carefully uttered the much-practiced translation of "Thank you for your help." The attendant snarled at me in response. Chalking that up to the palpable dislike for Americans I sensed from the woman, I waited my turn in line.

Opening the stall, I immediately noticed one thing was missing. The toilet. I looked down to see a bedpan tiled into the floor and bit back the bile rising in my throat. Beggars can't be choosers, so I did the best I could and then doused myself with half a bottle of hand sanitizer before returning to wait for our train.

Alex explained that we would be in first class, while he would be in third. He cautioned us to keep our valuables hidden, to never allow anyone but the porter inside the cabin, and to avoid the tea we'd be served if we wanted to sleep.

All first class is not created equal. Our cabin was a small

room with convertible benches along both walls with a square table in between. It was tight, but by the time the porter arrived to convert the benches into beds, I was so tired I didn't care. Bed is a generous description. I think an army cot is probably more comfortable than the flat, hard, narrow cushion placed across the bench. If this was first class, I could only imagine how Alex was doing in steerage.

Not to beat a dead horse, but the first-class bathroom was actually worse than the faculties at the train station. The bathroom had a narrow, stained sink and a hole cut in the floor open to the tracks below. Suffice it to say, it's obviously tough to aim on a moving train.

Exhausted, we slept for a few hours, and then watched the sunrise at two a.m. as the train chugged through the Russian countryside. A little after three a.m., we pulled into Kursk. I knew it was a town of approximately 400,000 people. In 2000, that was more than the populations of Newark, Las Vegas and Minneapolis. I expected to find a city; instead, I felt more like Laura Ingalls returning to Walnut Grove circa 1870. The cars were ancient, the roads were pitted and partially paved, and the houses looked as if they'd been built by small children out of whatever materials were handy at the time. Roofs were corrugated metal, peeling and plastered with melted hunks of tar retrieved from any one of dozens of potholes that turned the streets into slaloms.

There was one home on a corner that was large, impressive and fenced like a fortress. Alex explained it was the home of the local mafia boss. He seemed very proud of the fact that his own home was right up the street from mafia guy. His home was also guarded by an elaborate electric fence. It was a modest, two-story home on a half acre. Land ownership is a big thing to Russians, understandable given four hundred years of imperialist rule followed by seventy years of communism. The only problem, of course, is that in order to have electricity, a line would have to pass over a neighbor's property and that seemed to be an insurmountable problem. So, Alex was dependent on a generator and the sporadic delivery of electricity whenever his neighbor decided to share the electric pole.

Wearing shoes inside the home is strictly forbidden. Though the floor was dusty and dirty, as guests we complied. Besides, I was all set to take a nice hot bath. You guessed it, water was another issue. Like an old rerun of Green Acres, we had to pump water by hand. It was cold, unfiltered, and rampant with bacteria. One of our first responsibilities was to use our expensive camping bottles with the charcoal filters to keep from getting dengue fever or some other disease. The closest I got to a bath was standing in a metal basin and pouring frigid water over myself, one bottle at a time. With no electricity for my hair dryer or curling iron, I was afraid my new daughter would take one look at me and beg to stay in the orphanage.

Alex's mother served us giant bowls of soup. I recognized the cabbage, potatoes and onion, but the gray meat floating on top was a mystery. When I used my phonetic Russian to thank her for the food I merely pretended to eat, she laughed and shuffled off into the kitchen. She put my dish on the floor and, almost immediately, four dogs and three cats came scurrying over to devour the food I'd left behind. I was happy to supplement the diet of the mangy animals, until I realized there was no hot water, no dishwasher and no dish soap. The bowl was simply dunked in a bucket of standing water, and then placed in a drainer to dry. My cootie meter zoomed into the red zone.

My excitement overruled everything else as I put on 'the dress' and prepared to go to the orphanage. Luggage restrictions and carting all the 'gifts' severely limited what I could bring in the way of clothing. I had 'the dress,' one shirt, one pair of jeans, and a pair shorts. That was the sum total of my wardrobe.

Enter Vlad. He was our driver and apparently the go-to guy for the orphanage. He was 6'7" and reminded me of Lurch from the Adam's Family. He was just learning English, so we had some initial communication problems. What he did make clear was that our daughter was ill and before we could go to meet her, we needed to give him cash for medicine. What he couldn't make clear was what was wrong with her. So, after an hour's detour, we finally made our way to the outskirts of Kursk to what looked like a four-story factory. When I asked about the warehouse-like building with the frosted, reinforced windows, Vlad explained that it had been a factory, though with the language barrier, his explanations included the fact that at one time, the building had been used for fine dining. I believed the first claim, the second wasn't even a remote possibility. The language thing was definitely challenging.

My heart was racing and I was clutching my husband as we parked in the untended lot and walked toward the nondescript metal doors. It felt exactly like the day nearly fourteen years earlier when I'd entered the hospital to give birth to our son.

Vlad had us wait in the foyer of the dark building while he disappeared into one of the small offices. We heard babies crying, punctuated by the occasional giggle. The place smelled like a nursing home, ammonia masked by fruity industrial air fresheners.

Vlad came out once to get the bag of gifts. He was accompanied by a stern, solid woman with a scarf around her head and a stained apron over a drab gray dress. She glanced at us, then dug into the bag and retrieved the tubes of red lipstick. Only then did she smile. Only then did I notice that she was missing several of her teeth but the ones remaining were decorated with shiny gold caps.

She and Vlad spoke for several minutes before disappearing down a long corridor. A few minutes later, he returned holding the hand of a tiny little girl wearing a blue wool dress with her short brown hair drawn up in a huge tulle bow. Her eyes remained downcast and the closer she got to us, the more tightly she clung to Vlad.

The four of us, under the watchful eyes of the stern director, went inside what was called the playroom. Vlad stayed for a minute, coaxing the little girl out from behind his leg. This was my Katie Scarlett, the name we'd agreed upon. No, we weren't stripping her of her Russian heritage, we were giving her an American name since she was going to be an American citizen. Oh, and the orphanage records had about three different names on file and no one was one hundred percent sure what her Russian name had been at birth.

I was busy trying to find one toy with all its parts. My husband was already sitting on the floor, spinning a single block on a hole in the carpeting. Katie went to my husband, fascinated by the spinning block and by him. She sat on his leg and touched his glasses and the side of his face. I reached out and stroked her back and she about leapt through the ceiling. Switching legs, she continued to sit and play with my husband, but kept a wary eye on my every move. My husband could tickle her tummy, smooth her hair and even tap the tip of her little nose, all to her utter delight. If I so much as inched forward, she'd grab his neck and bury her face against his skin.

Thanks to our agency, I was fully prepared for her reaction. I knew that she would bond with my husband long before she bonded with me. She was accustomed to women, but men were such an oddity at the orphanage that it only made sense that she would find him fascinating. She was also disciplined by the women who ran the orphanage, so she looked at all women as potential disciplinarians.

It took the better part of two hours, but she finally got up the nerve to move close enough to explore my watch. Much to our mutual delight, she loved the fact that it played a song when one of the buttons was depressed. She amused herself for quite some time with that. I loved it, since it gave me an opportunity to touch her, to smell her and, hopefully, to alleviate some of her fears.

All in all, that first visit was a rousing success. Even though we knew we'd only be spending a few hours with her before our first court hearing, it was still incredibly painful when Director Sour Face yanked her up by one arm, pulling her back into the bowels of the orphanage.

Our next stop was the courthouse to file the adoption request. Oh, and to pass out the vodka and the silk scarf requested by the presiding judge and his secretary. We were told that due to the fact that we were taking an older child, and paying the penalty fees for our combined age, in all likelihood we'd be shown the courtesy of an expedited hearing. Yeah, well, no one told the vodka-swilling judge that. He was gruff and dismissive, even after I'd phonetically thanked him for his assistance. According to his secretary, we'd have his decision in a few days.

So, back to chez Alex we went. There was a lot of soup served and I was fast growing tired of 'the dress.' The only bright moments were the times we were allowed to visit with Katie. By the third day, Director Sour Face relented and allowed us to take Katie back to Alex's home, where we could play with her and treat her to fresh cherries off the tree in Alex's back yard. I later learned this was a huge mistake— they don't give the children any fruit at the orphanage.

I wondered why. Fruit is good for children, obviously,

and it certainly had to be better than the gruel I'd seen the children eating. When we returned to the orphanage with Katie's lips stained red from the cherries, a mini-international incident erupted. Okay, so I didn't understand what Director Sour Face was saying, but I instinctively knew I was in serious trouble. She railed for the better part of a half hour, and then Vlad turned and translated her diatribe into a single sentence: "She does not think you are a fit parent and may report you to the Minister of Education." (The Minister of Education is the Russian version of the head of Social Services.) No one ever explained to my why cherries were a no-no.

When all else fails, cry. I'll never know if Director Sour Face was swayed by my tearful apology, I just know it worked. She decided not to rat me out to the powers that be and allowed us—grudgingly—to continue our off-site visits with Katie.

Over the course of the next few days, Katie warmed up to us. We could coax half smiles from her and, though reservation shone in her pretty green eyes, she would willingly come to us and sit in our laps. What she wouldn't permit was hugs and kisses. At least not right away and definitely not from me. Katie far preferred Bob and by day four, she was responding to him without hesitation. At best, she tolerated me. It stung a little, but I also knew this was a probability with an older child. Patiently, I hung back, not wanting to smother or scare her. She had to make the first move. When she did, it brought tears to my eyes. On day five, she greeted me by yelling "Mama!" when I arrived at the orphanage.

Our visit that day was short, only because we had a court date scheduled. Because Katie's birth parents had long ago had their parental rights terminated and because of her age, there was a good chance the judge would grant our adoption and we could head home the next day.

In order to make a good impression on the judge, I put on 'the dress,' and did the best I could in terms of personal beautification sans hair dryer, curling iron, electricity and running water. I wanted to take Katie home and, frankly, I wanted the hell out of Russia. I was tired, dirty, and not exactly enamored of my rustic accommodations.

The courthouse, like everything else, was crumbling without the support supplied by a centralized, functioning government. The building was dark and dreary, and our first stop was the Minister of Education's office.

We were assigned a translator specifically for court, and she was a lovely young woman whose husband was off fighting in Chechnya. She was a teacher, though she hadn't received a salary for nearly a year. Her husband hadn't been paid either, some sort of snafu that she seemed to take in stride. When they were paid, their combined monthly income was roughly the equivalent of sixty U.S. dollars. Personally, if my husband was off fighting a war, rebellion, conflict or whatever sanitized name you want to use, I'd insist he at least be paid for his service. But that isn't the Russian mindset. Maybe it's because they have such a long history of waiting. Maybe it's because there really isn't anyone in charge. Whatever the reason, be it salary or food, Russians are patient and accepting of having to wait for even the most basic necessities.

Except for bribes. We weren't even allowed into the Minister's office until his secretary had checked to make sure the second round of Sky vodka, scarf and lipstick were present and accounted for. Satisfied that our gifts were as requested, we were ushered into the inner office. I got my first taste of Russian sexism. The official would only shake my husband's hand. Me? I was invisible. I was okay with it; after all, I was going to walk out of there with everything I needed to adopt my daughter and leave.

The Good, the Bad, and the Ugly

I expected questions, maybe some chitchat. Nope. We barely had time to sit before he stamped the papers and sent us on our way. I guess quality time with the vodka was more important than talking to prospective parents.

We had one last hurdle—the court appearance. It was scheduled for two p.m., so we went to a horrible little café with chipped, dirty china, where Alex sipped wicked strong coffee, while we tapped our toes waiting the hour until our appointment. During that hour, I noticed an odd juxtaposition. Russians, as a rule, are non-demonstrative. They do, however, love a good debate. At least it sounded that way as conversations heated and fists pounded tabletops. For a group that avoids hugs and handshakes, they apparently have no problem arguing in public.

Russians are like Europeans, only not. They linger over coffee or vodka and seem in no particular rush. They also seem oblivious to the state of their country. For whatever reason, they ignore the cracks in the sides of buildings, the missing hunks of sidewalks, and the stench of trash being burned. A half dozen cows being herded down the major thoroughfare didn't faze anyone but me. Emaciated dogs roam from trash pile to trash pile, ferreting out food scraps while dodging traffic and the circa 1930 trolleys that pass for a public transportation system in Kursk.

After what felt like an eternity, Alex waited for us to pay his bill, and then we headed back to the courthouse. Once we were there, the Minister's secretary came downstairs and pulled Alex and our interpreter aside. A sense of foreboding knotted my stomach. Even though I didn't understand a word, based on facial expressions, it didn't look good.

Finally, Alex came back and said the judge had put our hearing off for two hours. He suggested we go to the orphanage and visit with Katie to pass the time before our hearing. As soon as we were alone, I told my husband I thought something was wrong. On the ride to the orphanage, Alex had avoided making eye contact and, for the first time, he'd been almost chatty. Suddenly he was the Minister of Tourism for Kursk, pointing out landmarks and explaining their historical or cultural significance to the country and/or the people. As interesting as that was, it struck me as odd that he'd spent five days grunting monosyllabic answers to every question and now he couldn't seem to shut up.

We weaved through the streets of Kursk, ending up at the orphanage. Alex bounded from the car like an eager puppy. He and Director Sour Face had a brief, rushed conversation before Bob and I could reach the entrance. I was expecting something bad but, instead, they brought Katie to the playroom and we sat on the floor with the collection of broken toys. I began to relax, watching Katie play and thinking how cute she'd look in the outfit I'd brought for the trip home.

Katie was clinging to Bob's neck when Alex stuck his head in and told us it was time to go. As was our custom, Bob, with Director Sour Face close behind, carried Katie out to the parking lot so she could kiss us good-bye. In less than a week, she'd learned to giggle when showered with little flutter kisses and squealed with delight when Bob kissed one cheek while I kissed the other. She chanted Papa or Mama, randomly taking turns giving us hugs.

Director Sour Face reached into our little farewell ritual and practically yanked Katie out of Bob's grasp. It was so sudden that even Katie, who was far more accustomed to the rough treatment, seemed stunned. Director Sour Face and Alex talked briefly, and whatever they said in Russian made Katie cry. We'd never seen her cry before, but big tears spilled down her cheeks, and she stretched out her arms toward us calling, "Mama! Papa!"

"What is it?" I demanded of Alex.

"No more adoptions."

"What?"

"You must leave now."

My world was spinning. "She's upset," I argued, as Katie was whisked back inside the orphanage. "She needs us."

Alex shook his head. "No. You must leave. No more adoptions."

"You mean today, right?" I asked.

He shook his head. "No. Americans can't have Russian children. You must leave. Today."

There we were in that dismal, weed-infested parking lot, stunned stupid. We couldn't believe what was happening. I wanted to scream at them, explain that we'd already lost one child and couldn't bear to lose another. The orphanage was a hovel, home to 154 children all in desperate need of a family, and we were ready, willing and able to provide at least one of them with one.

Instead, Alex stuffed us in the car, took us to his house, had us pack, and we were unceremoniously taken to the train station. We couldn't reach our adoption agency, and Alex kept telling us that it was our fault. He insisted that one of the U.S. news magazine shows had run an expose on foreign adoptions and all but accused the Russian government of selling their children to desperate, selfish American couples.

When we reached the Moscow Sheraton, Alex dropped us like a bad habit. We finally reached our adoption agency and our agent told us that it was more likely that the Minister had simply denied our waiver request, and we'd be required to return in a few weeks or months to finalize the adoption.

Weeks? Months? How many? She hedged, explaining that our adoption hinged on the whims of the Russian government. We had no choice but to return home. That was probably the longest flight of my life. To make matters worse, several couples on the flight had their children in their arms. I was enveloped by the same emptiness I'd experienced after Kyle's death. Once again, I was a mother without a child.

We landed at Dulles International Airport, forgetting that it was Fourth of July weekend. The traffic added another three hours to the already hellishly long trip. We made a few calls to friends and family, letting them know we were back, but that we didn't bring Katie home. They were all sympathetic and offered encouraging words, but those words were lost in the quagmire of my personal despair.

My house never felt so empty. On Monday morning, I unpacked the cute outfit I'd bought to bring Katie home, returning it to the closet in the girly, pink desolate bedroom. Our agent called and insisted that this was nothing more than a minor setback. She felt certain that it would just be a matter of a few days before we could go back and get Katie.

I didn't believe her. Or, more honestly, I couldn't believe her. I was too afraid of having my hopes dashed again. I was afraid it would never happen. I was afraid, period. I started thinking about what I could do to fill the void of not being a mother. I wondered *if* I could.

I'd stopped writing and, frankly, had absolutely no interest in writing a happily-ever-after book. Or any other kind of book. I had trouble concentrating on anything aside from my own self-pity. I fell into the old habit of ignoring friends and family and wallowing in my pain and loneliness.

A week passed, then another, then another, then another and by the end of July, with no word and no hope on the horizon, I was obsessed with what might be happening to Katie. I doubted anyone had explained anything to her. She probably wondered why we so abruptly stopped visiting her.

My heart ached. Was she sick? Was she hungry? Was she lonely? The image of her tear-stained cheeks chased me to sleep every night.

The last week of July, I was off to the Romance Writers of America national conference. This annual event is usually a highlight, since it is the only opportunity I get to see certain friends. As the date grew near, I was paralyzed with fear. I knew my friends well enough to know that they'd rain gifts for Katie on me. They are a kind, generous group of women who had stood by me when Kyle was sick and then with me when he died. For some strange reason, I was convinced that they would grow tired of my life crises. I didn't think I could go and tell them that the adoption was on indefinite hold. I was so afraid of facing my friends with yet more bad news that I decided to cancel my trip.

As I reached for the phone, it rang. Our agency was calling to let me know that we needed to return to Russia for a hearing on August 21. We'd be required to stay for ten business days following the hearing. I was so excited I started to hyperventilate. I braced myself, certain there had to be a 'but' coming.

I was right. We had a firm hearing date, *but* the officials in Kursk wouldn't confirm that Katie was still at the orphanage. I didn't know whether to squeal with delight or scream from frustration. I called my husband and told him the news. Like me, he was cautiously optimistic. There was also a problem. As the department head at his college, he had to be on campus when classes started on the twenty-fifth of August. He could go to Russia for the hearing but he'd have to return early, which meant I'd have to bring Katie home by myself.

With tempered excitement, I attended my conference and, as I suspected, my friends threw a beautiful kid shower at the hotel. Katie had dozens of 'aunts' eagerly awaiting her arrival. By the time the conference was over, my excitement was no longer tempered. In fact, the support from my friends had actually buoyed my confidence to the point where I felt 99% sure this second trip to Russia would be a complete success.

So once again, I carefully packed for the long trip back to Kursk. As instructed, I packed food, drinks and clothing for Katie, as well as for myself. Not an easy task, given I was allowed a backpack and one small suitcase for a trip that would last anywhere from twelve to eighteen days.

Even if I was skeptical and jaded when we landed in Moscow, I still had a ribbon of hope wrapped around my heart.

We arrived a few hours before the evening train to Kursk. The ever-helpful (Not!) Alex greeted us at the airport—again with a sign that read 'Pollermo.' I asked him if he'd seen Katie at the orphanage and that seemed to annoy him. Apparently, as our host family, he didn't think it was in his job description to find out if the daughter we'd flown halfway around the world—twice—in order to adopt, was still in Kursk.

I didn't like Alex, and I sensed the feeling was mutual. He hosted adoptive families only because it filled his pockets with U.S. dollars. He claimed he was a physician, but since doctors are paid by the government, and the government hadn't been paying anyone but themselves for the better part of two years, he'd given up his practice. He now practiced non-traditional medicine in Kursk. Or, more accurately, he smashed what looked like berries and vinegar in a glass and sold it to his neighbors as some sort of cure-all. He also had some sort of machine that he tried to explain. If I understood correctly, it could 'sense' cancer in the body. Yeah, right. Acting as a host did more for Alex than just line his pockets. It gave him an excuse to travel to Moscow on someone else's dime.

The Good, the Bad, and the Ugly

Alex dragged us all around Moscow for the better part of a day. We thought he was killing time before the evening train. He waited until we were in a cab on the way to the train station before mentioning that we'd be catching the train outside. Um, huh? It was drizzling and, forget the date on the calendar, Moscow is cold even in the summer. Well, it turned out there was a bomb scare at the main station. Hundreds of commuters were huddled around the outside of the building.

Curious, my husband and I asked what the procedure was for a bomb scare. After all, a week earlier Chechynian rebels had reportedly blown up another Moscow train station. Bomb squad? Nope. Bomb sniffing dogs? Nope. Robotic probe? Nope. The procedure is to stand outside in case it blows up. Yep, that's the plan. Simple, ineffectual, but very, very Russian. We stood in the drizzle, leaning against the could-blow-up-any-second station and waited like everyone else by order of Alex. When the train arrived, we had to drag our modest luggage behind the building, jump down onto the tracks—being careful not to step on the 'hot' track—walk through waist-high weeds and then hoist ourselves up into the train. Alex didn't lift a finger to help. I guess it was hard on him, what with thousands of my dollars strapped to his waist.

First class wasn't available, so we traveled second class. Personally, I couldn't tell the difference. The room was still small and dank, and the bathroom was still a hole in the floor at the end of the car. We weren't offered any tea, but that was about it. Unlike our first trip, we were much more subdued and cautious. I think we both needed to know that Katie was still at the orphanage before we could muster our excitement.

By noon the next day, we were reunited with our daughter. We were thrilled to see her. She was not so thrilled to see us. Her little face closed up, and she watched us with hooded eyes as we swooped down to greet her. She cowered behind

Director Sour Face. Okay, I was discouraged. My daughter preferred the stocky, six-foot tall taskmaster to me. And not just me. She was equally leery of Bob, whom just seven weeks earlier she'd adored almost on sight.

The presents we'd left for her and the photo album we'd made showing her room and our home had all been stolen by the staff. Apparently they wanted albums and tossed the photos. We'd anticipated this and brought replacements. We also didn't begrudge the staff, they all had children at home and the toys, I'm sure, were well loved.

The final adoption hearing happened on August 21. We walked into the court holding hands and our breath. We had a different interpreter, a nice woman who walked us through the process. Bob and I were seated at a counsel table with the interpreter. A young woman sat at the opposite table, and we were told she was the attorney representing the government. A man we'd never seen before entered the courtroom and was called to stand in the well before the judge. A packet of papers was passed to us, written in Cyrillic. Then the questioning began.

I sat stunned, as the man told the judge the following:

The government had made every attempt to find a suitable Russian family to adopt the child.

The child suffers from learning and cognitive disabilities due to a bad mother (that was the translation).

The child has only one kidney and will require a lifetime of medical treatments.

The child has a simple mind (again, that was the translation).

The child cannot learn to speak (um, huh?).

The child can get special treatment in the United States.

The Good, the Bad, and the Ugly

As if to prove that the things he was telling the court were true, the translator kept tapping the file, drawing our attention to specific paragraphs. In a hushed whisper, I asked, "What are they talking about?"

The translator answered, "It has to be this way. The government prefers to allow adoptions when the child has retardation."

I was about to argue the point, when the translator shot me a warning look. I remembered my adoption agency telling me to keep my mouth shut, regardless of what I heard. So, I folded my hands in my lap and listened as the judge asked my husband—through the interpreter—if we were willing to accept this retarded child into our family. Hearing the word 'retarded' over and over made my blood boil, but I managed to keep my mouth shut. I kept reminding myself repeatedly that silence was the means to an end.

The only minor snag was a prolonged questioning about why I hadn't adopted my stepchildren. It took the interpreter quite a while to get the judge to understand that my stepchildren were thirty-four and thirty, and that they had a perfectly good mother in my husband's first wife. Yes, they were teenagers when we married, but under U.S. law, I couldn't adopt them. There was some irony in all this, given we have always had the kind of blended family that others envy. My husband's first wife spent holidays with us, and all the childhood milestones were shared events. My step-children never had to do the divorced-parents mambo, since we all got along so well. But there we were, in crumbling Kursk, trying to explain all this to a judge, who made it apparent he thought we were lying. Divorced people, in his opinion, were meant to be enemies.

I couldn't believe *that* was his sticking point. The debate dragged on for a good thirty minutes before he sighed heavily and, without warning, scrawled his name across the bottom of the adoption decree. Stunned and rigid, I felt my husband wrap his arms around me while the translator patted me on the back. It was over. The adoption was a done deal. Almost.

The judge had conditionally granted the adoption. It wouldn't become final until ten business days later. I was thrilled. My husband was thrilled. We wanted to celebrate. So did Alex, so he took us to a small coffee house. It was just after three, and Alex's idea of a celebration was doing shots of vodka. Secretly, I didn't think Alex needed an excuse to do shots, especially when I was paying for them, but for once, I didn't care.

I did want to go see Katie and tell her the news. Unfortunately, Director Sour Face prohibited all visits after two p.m. I had to contain myself until the next morning.

It was a very long night, made longer by the fact that The Creeper had made a special meal in honor of our semi-victory in court. The Creeper was Alex's mother. Alex never bothered to tell us her name, nor did she speak a word of English, so we'd given her that name because it fit. She was a tiny little woman, who was so stealthy, you never knew when you'd turn around and find her standing there. Doing some rough math, we figured she was maybe in her early fifties, but she looked more like eighty. Her skin was weathered and her hands were gnarled from years of manual labor. She rose early every morning and tended to the goat they kept in a small corral in their backyard. The rest of her day was spent digging potatoes and other vegetables that were stored in the vast root cellar beneath the house. She did all the cooking and waited on her son as if he were royalty.

In all my time in Kursk, I never witnessed Alex raise a finger to help his mother. It felt oddly as if I'd time travelled back to the 1950s. Except that the Creeper didn't wear pearls, pumps and a freshly pressed dress to do her chores. Then again, the Creeper had a broom fashioned from animal hair that had been tied to a stick and got her water from a hand-cranked pump in the backyard. Given her physically demanding, repetitive lifestyle, it was no wonder she looked thirty years older than her actual age.

Alex said she'd been a factory worker until the fall of communism. Since then she'd been unable to find work. He said it not with compassion, but with contempt. Alex didn't bother to mask his dislike of women. He was so snotty to his mother that I almost wished I'd taken the time to learn the phrase "your son is gay" phonetically. Seems the Creeper was the only one who didn't realize her son had a boyfriend in Moscow. Being on the down low in Russia is, to say the least, frowned upon.

Bob and I were all smiles as we sat down to the cabbage soup with the gray meatballs floating on top. Even knowing that Katie was practically ours wasn't enough to get me to eat the mystery meatballs.

That night we tried to sleep, sharing a well-worn twin bed with a lumpy, thin mattress. Not an easy task, since it gets dark at eleven and the sun rises at two a.m. Oh, and I learned something. The neighbor's roosters do not just welcome the break of dawn and then go silent. Nope, they cock-a-doodle-doo constantly.

I think I was also feeling a small sense of dread. Bob was leaving the next evening to return home for the start of the semester. I'm fairly well travelled, but my destinations normally included room service and fruity drinks with little umbrellas.

A little while after the sun rose, so did I. I'd begun a ritual. Before the Creeper or Alex got up, I'd go down to the kitchen and do my best to sterilize whatever I could. Like a heroin addict, I held a lighter under the spoons, hoping beyond hope I could kill some of the rampant bacteria. I'd boil some water on the stove and do my best to rinse the guest/dog bowls.

The Creeper would get up and, if it was working, turn on the circa-1960 black-and-white television for the latest news. It wasn't real news, at least not any kind I was used to. Putin had shut down the 'free' press, so all information was funneled through the government. That last morning Bob was there, the major breaking news story was the sinking of the Kursk submarine in the Baltic Sea.

The name thing is just a coincidence. The town of Kursk was the site of one of the largest tank battles of World War II. I'm just guessing here, but I'm thinking there's a pretty good chance that the submarine was named for the town.

Throughout the day, when the television worked, the Russian government was releasing all sorts of information. The submariners were safe and they had a plan to get them out of the sub. The Norwegians or the Swedes—don't recall which—had some sort of equipment that would allow them to lower a tube to the main hatch and the trapped men could escape. There were also reports that the sinking was the result of U.S. war games gone awry, and that the Americans were responsible for the sinking. Or maybe the British. One thing was constant, they assured the viewing public that the men were definitely still alive.

Bob and Katie and I had one more family visit before Alex escorted him back to Moscow. In the twenty-four hours I was alone with the Creeper, I read books. I'd long since finished the three I'd brought with me, so I was forced to choose from the books left behind by previous families Alex and the Creeper had hosted. I was introduced to the sub-genre of men's adventure. Or, as I like to think of them, fat, sweaty ugly guys get to have lots of sex with a tall, leggy blonde flight attendant who just happens to be standing at the edge of the jungle. No matter how gross and disgusting the man is/was/will be, said leggy blonde can't wait to share some alone time with him. I've been writing romantic suspense for more than fifteen years and, I've gotta tell you, I'm not sure why the romance genre gets a bad rap when it's men's adventure that _really_ requires some heavy-duty suspension of belief.

The next week and a half, I fell into a routine. Alex ignored me. The Creeper kept trying to get me to eat cat or whatever was in the served-three-times-a-day meal, driver and sometimes translator Vlad took me to the orphanage to visit with Katie or to pick her up and take her back to Alex's place.

It may have been the most difficult nine days of my life. Katie would wander around looking for Bob and she still preferred Vlad to me. Even though intellectually I knew there is rarely an instant bond between an adoptive mother and an older child, it still stung. 'Give it time, give it time,' became my mantra. Only selfishly, I didn't want to give it time. I wanted her to at least like me. Even just a little. Didn't happen though. The only time she'd give me a half-hearted hug was at Vlad's urging.

Even though the adoption was final, I still wasn't allowed to keep Katie overnight. It was hard to entertain a three-year-old day in and day out with nothing but some fruit snacks and small toys. I would have enjoyed taking her someplace to play, but I was told that since my husband was not in the country, my movements were restricted. I didn't have the authority to take Katie anyplace other than Alex's house.

Then again, there aren't too many places to take a child in Kursk. I only saw one grocery store with refrigeration. Other than that, all consumable items were sold at roadside stands. Meat lay in the sunshine next to eggs and fish. Even though I was perpetually hungry due to my refusal to eat the mystery meatball soup, I wasn't hungry enough to eat foods teaming with flies out in the open. Forget Jenny Craig™, eighteen days in Russia and I'd lost nearly fifteen pounds.

Finally, the day came for me to pick up Katie and say good-bye to Kursk. Everyone in the town seemed happy that day, mainly because the Russian news outlets were all announcing that the submariners had been rescued safe and sound. Me? I was fussing with the clothes I'd brought for my daughter.

At seven o'clock, I was allowed to go to the orphanage to pick up Katie for the all-night train to Moscow. It was the first step toward home. For the first time, I was allowed up to the sleeping area. The beds were pine rectangles with thin mattresses, and they slept three or four to a rectangle. The sides of the rectangles came up a few feet; I suppose that was a safety feature. All the children were naked.

Sour Face handed Katie to me naked. I dressed her in the cute Gymboree outfit and matching shoes. She wasn't as fascinated by the dress as she was the shoes. She kept rubbing them and exploring the stitching and the decorations. Unbeknownst to me, it was only then that she was told by Vlad and Sour Face that she was leaving forever. She seemed stunned by the news, but she waved to the other 153 children as we left.

Once we boarded the train, Katie and I were alone for the very first time. She was terrified and mesmerized. She'd never seen a train. Never seen streetlights. When the porter turned our benches into beds for the night, she was fascinated and kept trying to open the compartment to see what else might be inside.

Using my horrible phonetic Russian, I asked her if she had to go to the bathroom. She did, but she didn't want any part of holding my hand as we walked down the hall to the bathroom. The minute she saw the hole in the floor and the tracks beneath, she refused to step inside. Prepared, I had some pull-ups, so I pulled those on and asked the nice lady in the next cabin—who'd already spoken to me in English— to explain their function.

Katie wasn't thrilled with the idea. Instead, she wanted a chamber pot like the one they had back at the orphanage. I never thought about that, so she was out of luck.

I was exhausted, but Katie didn't show the first signs of tiring. Even after I tucked her in, I could see her eyes wide open as she watched a new and unfamiliar world whoosh by out the large window in our cabin.

She never did sleep, nor did I, but that didn't matter as soon as I recognized that we had arrived in Moscow. Again, Alex proved to be useless. I had a backpack, a small rolling suitcase and carried Katie while he walked in front of me through the terminal to where a car waited for us. I felt like a Sherpa and, not so quietly, cursed his uselessness.

After battling morning rush hour in the drizzle, we finally arrived at the Sheraton, where I was immediately asked to surrender my passport to the desk clerk. Alex couldn't seem to explain why they needed my passport, as well as Katie's, in order for us to spend the night, but I was hardly in a position of bargaining power.

Alex informed me that in accordance with Russian law, I had to take Katie to a doctor for a medical clearance, and then to the U.S. Consulate to get her exit VISA. We'd taken care of procuring her passport in Kursk. He handed me a piece of paper with three U.S. approved doctors on it, and I selected the one closest to the hotel.

We had about an hour to kill before we had to leave for the doctor's office, so Katie and I explored our room. For her, the highlight was the flushing toilet. She'd never seen a real toilet, so the novelty of watching water swirl and drain was riveting. The only downside was that I was taking a quick shower and, every time she flushed, the water turned ice cold. Even at my skankiest, I was still in better shape than ninety percent of the people in the street. I stood out as if I had a big, flashing neon sign over my head telling the world I was an American in Moscow adopting a child.

Putting 'the dress' back on, I dried my hair, applied makeup and felt more human than I had in seventeen days. I made a futile attempt to call Bob, but couldn't seem to get past the hotel operator.

My jaw started to hurt and I thought it was from lack of sleep, nutrition, or whatever. I took a couple of Tylenol, then stuffed some dry cereal and a couple of juice pouches into the backpack. I wanted to be prompt, since I was sure I'd hear about it if Alex had to wait a nanosecond.

I'd been warned not to open the hotel door to anyone other than Alex. And he even suggested that I wedge the chair under the door for added security. I was not feeling relaxed. But at least I was clean.

Alex was half an hour late and, as was his custom, didn't so much as offer an apology. Or any help. Instead, he power walked out of the hotel. Easy for him, since he wasn't carrying a backpack and a twenty-three-pound child. Alex took us on a brisk walk through the drizzle, and down a creepy side street to an unmarked door. I noticed that the drizzle left my arms dotted with black soot and dirt. Pollution is a problem in Moscow. One of many as I was about to learn.

The doctor's office—and I'm being seriously generous here—was two rooms with peeling plaster walls and cracked tile floors. Something green and fuzzy was growing in the grout. The exam room reminded me of the doctor's office circa 1880 on display at the Smithsonian. Alex didn't accompany us inside.

I sat on a round stool with a cracked leatherette seat and let Katie have the run of the eight-by-five room. She enjoyed opening and closing the sparsely stocked drawers. By that point, I was too tired to care and hardly in a position to discipline a child who clearly wasn't all that fond of me. My jaw started to throb, but I chalked it up to exhaustion.

An hour and a half later, a man in a pristine lab coat entered the room. He smiled at me, which made me feel good, since I'd been subjected to Alex's snarls for so long. Katie smiled at him and practically jumped into his arms. Even though I knew intellectually that her reaction was normal, I felt a stab of jealousy.

The doctor introduced himself in perfect English. He offered me his hand and, still smiling, said, "Give me fifty dollars U.S. or I won't sign her health certificate."

Apparently, our Glasnost moment was over. Being between a rock and a Russian place, I dug into my backpack and pulled out one of my four remaining fifty-dollar bills. Once he had his 'bonus,' since I had to pay another hundred for the examination, he told me to take Katie's clothing off.

After prying her from the doctor's leg, I removed her cute little sweater, overall dress, matching top and panties. Then I reached for her shoes and all hell broke loose. She reared back and spit in my face, then jerked away from me and went to stand behind the doctor. Wiping the spit from my cheek, the same cheek that was throbbing with a dull ache emanating from my jaw, I could only look at the doctor and ask if he could skip a foot check.

I wanted to cry and scream and cry some more, but that wasn't an option. After the medical exam, I was expected to go to the US Consulate to apply for the final VISA that would allow Katie and me to get on our scheduled flight home the next afternoon.

Doctor Had-His-Handout spent five minutes—if that—doing the exam, then signed off on my paperwork. One hurdle down, one more to go. Alex was in the waiting room, sipping a cold soda, reading the newspaper.

I'd been shaken down and spit on, so my patience with his snotty attitude was wearing thin. The Consulate, he explained, was a mile away, an easy walk. All we had to do was swing by the hotel to reclaim our passports. A four-block detour, he announced, was a minor inconvenience—for him. I lost it. I told him the only way I was walking a mile plus a detour in the rain was if he carried the kid or the backpack. Pick one. He took the backpack and punished me by walking faster than normal.

A line of Russian citizens circled the block around the Consulate, but as a U.S. citizen, I was immediately let inside. I found myself in a comfy room with fifty other people, all with children ranging in age from infant to maybe twelve. There was coffee and water and cookies.

Karma is a wonderful thing. Alex wasn't allowed in the American room. I secretly hoped he was sitting on some hard floor, cooling his jets while I chatted with my fellow Americans. It was a happy place.

We were all becoming parents and talking about going home and starting our new lives with our children. People shared the stories that had led them to this path. Most were infertile couples, but there were a handful of people who had other children at home—biological and/or adopted—and a few who had empty nests and had decided to start over again.

I don't know why, but I didn't tell my new temporary friends my own story. Maybe I didn't want to get 'the look.' When someone hears you've lost a child, they instantly look at you with a mixture of pity and relief. They're genuinely sorry for your loss, but secretly (and appropriately) thinking, "Thank God it wasn't my kid."

There was, however, a great deal of discussion about my rapidly swelling jaw. One of the dads waiting his turn happened to be a dentist. He suggested I might have developed an abscess. Great, just what I needed. My spirits plummeted. I still had thirty-six hours before I'd be back home. Then I remembered that part of our kit from Passport Health Services included some antibiotics. I'd take some when I got back to the hotel and, hopefully, stave off the infection.

There was no way I was going to seek medical attention in Russia. Especially not of the dental variety. I'd spent a lot of my time with Katie trying to scrape the black plaque off her teeth with my fingernails. In her three-and-a-half years, she'd never seen a toothbrush. The novelty of it amused her, though the actual process of brushing wasn't as much fun for her as pretending it was some sort of paintbrush.

Finally, my name was called and I corralled Katie, who'd been playing with another child on floor. She was not happy when I picked her up to take her to the counter. I didn't know if it was because I was holding her—not her favorite thing— or because she just didn't want to abandon her newfound friend. I did know she responded by spitting in my face. Again. We definitely needed to work on that.

Sitting Katie on the counter, I passed our papers to the attendant. He was about my age and looked totally bored as he moistened his fingertip and flipped through my passport. His head came up and he asked, "You aren't, by any chance, from Crofton, Maryland, are you?"

Crofton is a small town just north of Annapolis. Blink and you miss it. I'd mostly grown up there and mostly avoided it after graduating from college. "Yes," I said, my eyes dropping to his name badge. I recognized the surname. He was one of six or seven brothers who'd lived in a house around the corner from mine. I wasn't sure if he was the one in my high school graduating class, but it didn't matter. He was the first genuinely friendly face I'd seen in weeks, and if there hadn't been a glass partition between us, I'd have kissed him on the lips with tongue.

Breaking with protocol, he stamped my papers right then and there, eliminating the return trip the next morning. I had Katie and I had official clearance.

When I left the Consulate with papers in hand, Alex accused me of bribing an official. As much as I tried to explain that the adoption gods had smiled on me, he insisted in berating me all the way back to the hotel. I told him I was going to my room to see if I could arrange for an immediate flight out.

He just snickered and said, "Not the Russian way."

I was undaunted.

I was an idiot. Apparently, it took a Papal Dispensation to change a flight. I was stuck in Russia for another day. Dejected, I dug into the backpack for the emergency kit from Passport Health. Someone—either customs or Alex, or one of his family members—had stolen the antibiotics. Katie, who until that moment hadn't spoken a single word to me, started saying 'Beet, cooshit." My phonetic Russian was enough to let me know she was telling me she was hungry and thirsty. Since I was running low on juice pouches and snacks—Alex's nephew had helped himself one day when I was at the orphanage—I figured we'd go down to the restaurant and eat a real meal.

But first, I wanted to try to reach my husband again. I got lucky, and the call went through. Just hearing his voice

The Good, the Bad, and the Ugly

made me cry. I recapped my adventures, successes, failures and frustrations. He was so sweet and encouraging. I knew he wanted to be with me, but as it turned out, it was serendipitous that he was at home. He'd call my dentist and make arrangements for an emergency appointment the day after I got home.

I didn't want to hang up, so I told him all about the television that had one channel dubbed in German, but that if I turned the volume up loud enough, I could hear the English. Oh, and the newspapers were recounting the heroic rescue efforts to save the Kursk submariners. He informed me that the uncensored news had pronounced them all dead days ago. There was no rescue mission taking place. So much for Putin's reputation as a progressive. In mid-sentence, the line went dead.

I took Katie down to the restaurant on the lobby level. It was a pretty typical Sheraton dining room. White table clothes, pretty stemware, silverware and candles in the center of each table. The hostess greeted us with a smile and showed us to a table in the center of the room. I sat Katie in the chair. She immediately slid down, taking the tablecloth with her. Glasses and plates shattered, utensils went flying and I bent down to try to capture her.

The action made my jaw hurt so much that I literally saw stars. She managed to destroy two more tables before I got her around the waist and lifted her up and away from further destruction. The hostess and a very unhappy-looking man I assume was the manager came running. They spoke in raised voices, and then the hostess told me the damage would be charged to my room.

I gave them my room number and asked the hostess to ask Katie what she wanted to eat. I placed an order and asked that it be delivered to my room along with some extra ice for my jaw. Thirty minutes later, a plate of chicken tenders and french fries arrived. Kate used them as drumsticks. I took a bite, then had her do the same thing. She spit it on the floor. At a loss, I called room service and explained the problem. Their response was that she'd probably never seen, let alone tasted, anything fried. They'd send up mashed potatoes and some soup. Great, problem solved.

The food arrived and there must have been five pounds of potatoes in a huge bucket and enough soup for ten. A huge problem, because Katie didn't have an 'off button' when it came to food. I knew this because I'd witnessed a meal at the orphanage. As soon as a child could hold a bowl, they were expected to get in line and fend for themselves, filling their bowls with whatever was in the massive pot. If you happened to be one of the last in line, the pickings were awfully slim. The result was, Katie would eat until she made herself ill. If it was on the plate or in a bowl, she'd eat it all or gag trying.

After seeing her gorge herself in a matter of minutes, I made a grab for the tray. We had a brief struggle before I was able to get it away and lift it high above her grasp. So now I had this heavy tray balanced precariously up in the air. I had a chair wedged under the door, and I somehow managed to put the tray in the hallway without Katie escaping. It took some doing, but I finally got the job accomplished and the chair secured back in place. A minute later, Katie had yanked the chair free and was turning the antiquated lock.

"Ne-yet, nee-a-nada," I said phonetically. I'd gotten that one right and, miraculously, she followed my instruction to stop what she was doing.

Neither of us had slept in nearly twenty-four hours. I figured a nice warm bath and more teeth brushing might tucker her out. If nothing else, she'd be clean. She liked the bathtub. She was particularly fond of taking handfuls of water and dumping them onto the bathroom floor. I quickly made a levy with bath towels and fully expected a call from the front desk telling me I was flooding the floor below. They'd probably put the floor on my bill as well.

I was at the I'm-so-tired-I-don't-care stage. Once she was pruney and the water was chilly, I reached in and pulled the stopper. Huge mistake. She screamed and climbed over the side, probably terrified that she'd be sucked down with the water.

I felt horrible. I kept forgetting that this little girl was in a whole new world and a lot of it was scaring her. I wanted so much to hold her and stroke her hair, but she still didn't want much to do with me. She did like her new pink pajamas but insisted on putting her shoes back on. Fine by me. I took her over to the window and pointed to the Moskva River. It was brown and murky, but I could show her boats and the rain and the sky, repeating every word over and over so she'd get more comfortable hearing the language and the sound of my voice.

When she seemed bored, I took her over to the bed and pulled out the small doll and the shape ball. She liked putting the shapes in the ball, and then when she grew bored, she stripped the doll. Well, except for the shoes. The girl had a serious thing about shoes.

I tried to lay with her, but that wasn't an option. The minute I laid down, she got out of the bed. I got up and tucked her in, then took the lumpy futon. I had to remake the bed so I could lie on my left side, since the right side of my face was sore and still swelling. Oh, the ice I asked for? They sent me four cubes.

When I saw she wasn't nodding off to sleep, I was literally pinching myself to stay awake, afraid she'd make another try for the door. She might be tiny, but she was strong and determined. After about an hour, her little lids started to flutter. She was just about to drift off, when someone began pounding on the door. She shot up like a rocket.

Going to the door, I squinted through the peephole and found a man dressed in an ill-fitting suit on the other side. "Yes?" I asked.

He flashed some sort of badge I was pretty sure was made of plastic and, in thickly accented English, said, "Ministry of Education. I must inspect the child."

Forewarned, I refused in pretty strong, colorful language. If I'd have opened the door, I have no doubt he would have taken Katie and demanded money to give her back. Instead, the only thing he got from me was explicit instructions on how to have sex without a partner.

However, the sixty-second power nap had revitalized Katie. It took me another bath and two hours of looking at boats and playing shapey ball before she finally dozed. I don't think I slept, it was more like I drifted in and out, alert to every noise.

At six the next morning, I ordered Katie some oatmeal and told her all about going to the airport and taking a plane and seeing papa.

"Papa?" she'd repeat, her expression no longer guarded as she'd look at the door, probably expecting him to show up, disappointed when he didn't materialize.

On the plus side, when I took her food away after she'd eaten at least a gallon of oatmeal, she didn't spit on me. Maybe I was making headway. She mimicked me as I brushed my teeth, fascinated when I'd wince and say, "Ouch!" whenever I got too close to the festering infection in my gums.

Her first official word—other than mama and papa—was 'ouch.' And I loved hearing it. It was progress.

I'd bought one of those kiddy leashes, knowing we'd be

standing in the Custom's line for hours, and even though she was terribly underweight, even she would get heavy after a while. One end has a loop, the other has a Velcro attachment you can keep your child tethered. Given Katie's proclivity for darting off, I dug it out of the suitcase and tucked it into the outer pocket of the backpack. As ordered, Katie and I went down to the lobby at exactly eight a.m. With the backpack on my shoulder, I was rolled the suitcase with one hand and had a firm grip on Katie's wrist.

Alex, who I'm pretty sure had spent the night with his secret lover, was waiting impatiently at the registration desk. I was going home with my daughter, and I refused to let him mess with my mood. Three hours, and we'd be aboard an Aeroflot jumbo jet heading home.

After paying for the room, food and an extra hundred for the dining room destruction, our passports were returned and we headed out to where the hired car was idling. The driver didn't budge from behind the wheel, popping the trunk from the inside, so I was left to juggle Katie, the back-pack and the suitcase. I was floored when Alex reached for my small suitcase. It was his first and only gallant gesture.

Wrong again. He started to unzip my suitcase. "What are you doing?" I asked.

"You take this to agency. More children," he said as he stuffed a small video cassette in with my clothes and toiletries.

Katie was jerking my arm, desperate to be set free on the streets of Moscow. I kept my hold. "I'm not allowed to take videos of the children or the orphanage," I reminded him. I was specifically told that taking videos was against the law. No wonder, since the conditions in Russian orphanages weren't exactly a shining example the Russians would want shared with the world.

"You take," he repeated. "First twenty minutes Russian

countryside. No one will know."

"I'll know," I told him.

"No matter." He rezipped the suitcase and tossed it inside the trunk, then slammed it.

Katie bit my hand.

"Ouch!" I cried.

"Ouch!" she repeated happily.

I couldn't fight them both, so I let the videotape thing go and scooped Katie up in my arms. Sliding over, Alex got in, and then glared at me when I planted Katie between us. It wasn't a long ride to the airport, but I didn't want her within reach of the handle, terrified she'd open the door and tumble into the clogged, congested downtown traffic.

Sheremetyevo International Airport is a large, busy heavily guarded airport. There are lots of young men in uniform carrying big guns. Alex's responsibilities to me ended at the entrance. As a Russian citizen, he was not allowed beyond the ticket counter. I managed a very insincere 'thank you' and followed the arrows to Customs. I had intended to open my suitcase and ditch the videotape at the first opportunity, but everywhere I looked, guards and military officers stood watch.

I joined about a hundred other international travelers, pulled out the kiddy leash and Velcroed it to Katie's wrist. She promptly tore off the Velcro and started to run. I didn't have time to pull the handle, so I carried my suitcase and caught up to her after a few strides. I also lost my place in line.

New tactic—Katie liked fruit snacks, so I pulled a bag out of the backpack and wiggled it in front of her. She made a grab for it, but I kept hold, giving her one at a time, using them like pet treats as we moved sluggishly forward. When I ran out of fruit snacks, I gave her my wallet and let her play with the coins. When that no longer held her interest, I had no choice but to pick her up and struggle to keep hold of her. Of course, she kept saying, "Ouch!" This didn't exactly endear me to the other travelers.

I got within two people of clearing Customs, when a guy who looked about nineteen tapped me on the shoulder. He was dressed in the burgundy-and-white uniform of the Russian army, and one gangly hand rested on some sort of automatic weapon. He said something to me in Russian. Whatever it was made Katie go still.

"I'm sorry," I said. "I don't understand."

"Come."

Oh crap, this couldn't be good. He led me around the Customs booth, took me down a corridor, and pointed to an empty office. Once we were inside, he took my documents, backpack and my suitcase and closed the door without further explanation. Katie grabbed the pencils out of a cup on the sparse desk and began breaking them into pieces. Me? I was sweating bullets and, being a writer, began to plot out my future.

The scene in my head began with Alex making a call to the authorities. The videotape had been a setup, because I hadn't cow towed to the little weasel. He'd set me up, and I was destined to spend the rest of my days in some freezing gulag on the tundra. Katie would go back to that horrible orphanage, and Bob would grow old never knowing what happened to me. I literally worked myself into hyperventilating as I watched the minutes tick off the clock. My flight was due to leave in an hour; then forty-five minutes; then thirty.

Then, with fifteen minutes to spare, the pencil-necked army guy came back, handed me my stuff and boarding passes, and then escorted me to the gate. Not a word was exchanged. Fine by me, I quickly put Katie in her seat and stowed my suitcase and backpack in the overhead bin. Katie was thrilled with the seatbelt and the headphone jack. I hoped the hum of the engine might lull her to sleep. But mostly I just hoped the plane would take off on time. The writer in me crafted another scene, whereby the Russian equivalent of SWAT stormed the plane and dragged me off kicking and screaming for parts and places unknown.

When the engines started, I let out a long, slow breath and my fear leached out like a balloon with a slow leak. It wasn't until we'd taxied down the runway, lifted off and I heard the landing gear hide in the fuselage that I really relaxed. Home. I was finally going home.

The fourteen-hour flight was uneventful and, thanks to the tri-lingual flight attendant, Katie got drinks, food, coloring books, and three sets of headsets—she kept snapping the plastic parts in two. She did everything but sleep. I didn't understand how such a tiny child could keep moving on less than seven hours of sleep in two days. If I didn't think she might storm the cockpit, I would have dozed. I was eating Tylenol like breath mints and holding an ice pack to my face for much of the trip. The ice helped. By the time we landed in New York, I looked semi-human.

I don't know what I'd been expecting, but it sure wasn't the long trek to Customs required before I could board the little crop duster that would take us to our final destination, Baltimore-Washington International. Following the signs, I held one side of the rolling suitcase and Katie held the other. We walked and walked and walked until we reached a very steep escalator heading down. I stepped on and only then realized that, never having seen one, Katie stood frozen at the top of the escalator. I turned, fully intending to scale my way back up to her, when a man in a business suit grabbed her like a football and brought her down with him.

When we met at the base of the escalator, he handed her to me. Or at least he tried. Katie got a death grip around his neck and made it clear she preferred to stay with the stranger. I pried her free and yes, she spit in my face again.

We then went into a small room where Katie's passport and documentation would be checked by U.S. Customs officials. I was getting excited. My plane was leaving in less than an hour, and it was only a thirty-five-minute flight. I was literally counting the minutes until we'd be reunited for the first time as a real family.

Yeah, well, about fifty other people had the same idea. As instructed, I took a number. Like some sort of deli line at a grocery store, a red board indicated they were currently serving number seventy-one. I was holding a ticket with the number one hundred thirty-three. Making that flight home wasn't looking so good.

As I watched the red numbers move at a snail's pace, Katie had finally reached critical mass. Lack of sleep, too much new stimulation and too many new people all combined, and she erupted into a ball of bad behavior. She made it clear she wanted out of the room and away from me. When that didn't happen, I was spat on, *again*. And bitten, *again*. Then she turned on fellow immigrants. She yanked a barrette out of one woman's hair, took another woman's purse, and when I instantly nixed that behavior, she went to our backpack, unzipped it, and dumped the contents on the floor. While I was chasing a tube of lip balm before it could go under a chair, she was unzipping the suitcase and dumping it out as well.

At that instant, sleep deprived, in pain from the abscess and just generally exhausted, I had trouble fighting back tears. And not because representatives from nearly every country on the Ivory Coast were checking out my undies and everything else that had tumbled from the suitcase. No, I was completely past caring. It was the angry, detached look in my daughter's eyes as she glared at me. At any moment, I expected her head to spin around on her shoulders. Any idyllic fantasies I had harbored about bonding with my daughter evaporated. If this was going to work, as I desperately wanted it to, I suspected we had a long road ahead of us.

Doubt, fear, and anxiety settled in the pit of my stomach. What I feared most, but never told a soul, not even my husband, happened. I questioned my decision to adopt. What if we never bonded? What if she spent the rest of her days looking at me as if I was the enemy? It happened. I'd read the articles, and it isn't as if the process lent itself to helping form an attachment. Adoptive parents are given only limited access and time with their children prior to leaving the country. I'd read the other articles too, the ones where bonding never happened; families and marriages crumbled under the strain of having a child who never adjusted. This problem is magnified when adopting an older child.

On the plus side, I was so deep into my funk that I didn't realize it was seventeen minutes before my flight was due to take off, and I was still two numbers away from my turn. Under normal circumstances, I would have picked up my cell phone and called my husband or a friend. I needed someone to boost my dashed hopes and dreams. Unfortunately, I'd been denied my request to take a cell to Russia, so I couldn't call anyone without leaving the room to use the payphone. Leaving the room meant giving up my place in line, and that wasn't an option.

With eleven minutes to go, we went into Customs. Katie was fingerprinted and her documents checked. Well, checked might be a stretch. They got a cursory glance by the officer.

"I'm in a hurry," I said, my voice hoarse from lack of sleep and an excess of pent up emotion.

"And?" he grunted.

"My flight is about to leave."

"Life's tough that way," he said without looking at me. He pounded two ink stamps. One on Katie's passport and the other on the seal of the envelope containing all the official adoption papers. He passed them to me and called, "One thirty-seven!"

Guess I was done. I grabbed the backpack, the suitcase and Katie and started racing toward our gate, Inconveniently located in another terminal. By the time I reached the check-in desk, it was four minutes past the scheduled departure time. Sitting Katie on the counter and blocking any escape routes with my body, I dug out our boarding passes and asked the attendant what time the next flight was due to leave. The one thing working in our favor was that shuttles ran between JFK and BWI every hour or so. Even though I'd missed my flight, it was early afternoon so, hopefully, I had plenty of alternatives.

"Your flight hasn't left yet," she explained. "There's a mechanical problem. We're working on it now."

I wanted to sing the Hallelujah chorus. "Can we still board?"

She nodded and pointed toward a doorway open to a set of stairs. "Right down that way."

I hope I said 'Thank you,' but I can't honestly remember.

Carrying Katie and the stuff, I went down two flights of stairs and found myself in a lounge area. Passengers mulled around, chatting on phones, working on laptops or pacing the worn linoleum flooring. Me, I honed in on the pay phone and vending machines and went to them as if caught in a tractor beam.

As much as I wanted to call my husband, I knew I needed something to hold Katie's attention. Food would do it. I got a bag of cheese crackers and a bottle of water for her. I, the biggest Diet Coke™ junkie on the planet, had gone weeks without a fix. Aeroflot had the other major soda, but I'm a purest. I gulped that first slug of ice cold Diet Coke™ and felt a calm wash over me. I was one with my caffeine and aspartame.

After putting Katie in a chair with food and drink, I went to the pay phone to call my husband to hear his voice and to let him know that we'd be taking off half an hour late. He sounded giddy at the prospect of being reunited with his wife and new daughter. I couldn't dash his enthusiasm by telling her there was a tiny possibility that we'd adopted a spitting, biting version of the Spawn of Satan. I still clung to the last shreds of hope that once we got home, things would settle down and we'd be a 'normal' family. Drawing strength from the sound of my husband's voice was cut short when Katie got off the chair to go inspect a man using his laptop.

I was a half step away when she reached out and started tapping the keys. I braced myself, expecting the business-suited man to light into me.

"Ne-yet, nee-a-nada! Ne-yet, nee-a-nada!" I yelled as I grabbed her by the waist and yanked her away from the gentleman. To him, I gushed apologies and explained why I had practically zero control over my own child.

"Don't worry about it," he said after looking at me.

I think my swollen face, red eyes and skanky appearance earned me some sympathy points. Not only did Laptop Man not bite my head off, he helped me with my backpack and luggage when we were called out to the plane. Like prisoners called to a meal, we followed a yellow stripe painted on the tarmac to a small plane parked about ten yards from the building.

The steps were narrow, so even though the man had my backpack, I still had to climb the steps holding Katie in one arm, while lugging the suitcase behind me. It was September 2 and the air was thick, humid and super-heated by the plane's engine. The interior of the small plane was stuffy and perspiration clung to me. Katie's hair was wet with sweat and her little cheeks turned bright red. I opened the vent, but only a weak stream of warm air spewed from the vent.

The pilot came on and explained that the mechanical difficulty that had delayed takeoff was a full failure of the air-conditioning system. Instead of waiting for a replacement plane, he said that once we reached ten thousand feet, the plane would cool off on its own. He did tell people they were free to get off if they wished to wait for the next shuttle.

I groaned as two couples took the captain up on his offer. It took them several minutes to gather their things and exit through the small door. Then the plane taxied down the runway. As promised, the interior cooled off a few minutes after we were airborne. Katie was looking out the window and starting to fidget, so I bent down and started digging through the backpack for the shapey ball. By the time I retrieved it, she was fast asleep.

I couldn't believe it. The kid hadn't slept for days, and now she was out like a light. And within twenty minutes, the captain came on to tell us we were beginning our decent into BWI. In a matter of minutes, the plane bounced on the runway, and then slowly meandered to the terminal.

This being pre-September 11, as soon as the door opened, I saw my husband come racing out onto the tarmac to greet us. "Katie," I whispered. Nothing. I said her name louder. Nothing. Finally, I put the backpack on my shoulders, yanked the suitcase out from under the seat, pulled up the telescoping handle, then unhooked her seatbelt and lifted her sleeping body. I was dead on my feet, and she was dead weight.

The minute I appeared on the top step of the plane, Bob

came and took Katie from me, showering her sweaty face with kisses. She woke up and looked at him, then offered a small, cautious smile.

Inside the terminal, family and friends waited with balloons and flowers and gifts and tears. There were hugs and joy, as Katie was passed from person to person. No matter who was holding her, her green eyes remained fixed on Bob.

The airport gathering had been prearranged. We'd explained to everyone that, according to our agency, too much stimulation would be difficult for Katie, so the plan was that Bob and I would take her home, and our family would wait an hour or so before joining us.

Putting her in a car seat was an adventure. And ineffectual. I'd snap her in, and as soon as I slipped the last buckle into place, she'd start releasing the harness. After three frustrating attempts, I told Bob to get in the back seat with her and I'd drive home. That worked. With Bob as her companion, she was content to remain strapped in place.

I don't know whether it was the power nap on the plane or just the newness of the situation, but Katie's introduction to her new home went smoothly and relatively well. Simple things fascinated her. The refrigerator, the stove, the bathrooms and her room. She was most excited when we opened the closet and discovered three more pairs of shoes. Immediately she sat down and gave them all a try, eventually opting for the tennis shoes she'd been wearing almost every second since leaving the orphanage.

My parents, sister and her family came over at dinner time, bringing dinner with them, which was a great help and really appreciated. By now, I was nearing ninety-six hours with little more than catnaps as fuel. The swelling of my face had ballooned and the pain was pretty bad. My wonderful dentist had called in a prescription and Bob had it waiting for me.

Dinner was an adventure.Katie had texture issues, so the Chinese buffet didn't appeal to her at all. In the end, I made some instant mashed potatoes and microwaved some spinach. The spinach was a huge hit. She ate the entire package and three servings of potatoes. Apple juice was another hit, but her first taste of ice cream ended up unceremoniously spit on the floor. In addition to texture, she didn't like anything cold.

My family left just after seven and, after a bath, we switched to a new pair of pajamas—another hit—and to avoid a battle I was too exhausted to fight, put her shoes back on before tucking her into her bed. I stood in her doorway and listened as Bob read her *Madeline.* Her eyes were wide open and she took the book from him, flipped it back to the first page and handed it back to him. He started to read the story again. *Madeline* might not be lulling her off to dreamland, but it was working wonders on me. I went in to kiss Katie good night and, as I leaned down, she shoved me away. Not exactly a great start.

Traci Hall

CHAPTER THREE

The Good, The Bad and the Ugly

Everybody Has an Opinion

Good news was that by the end of the week, I was loaded with options. I could marry my underage sort-of boyfriend—who I genuinely cared about—but to be hitched together forever? Be real!

I could see it now. Me, those thousand babies, and a snoring drunk guy on the sagging couch. No way.

My mom was about to embark on marriage numero tres, when the ones before hadn't been too great. It was a risk I wasn't prepared to take.

Why add marriage, another sure mistake, to the giant heap of mistakes I'd already made? Being forced to be with someone just because it was the right thing to do didn't seem like the best plan for either Ricky or myself, let alone an innocent baby.

What would we do for money? Panhandling was not only illegal, but you didn't get much. Certainly not enough for rent, probably not even enough for Pampers. He didn't have a car, or insurance, or any type of stability.

Neither did I.

The Good, the Bad, and the Ugly

My job at Newberry's didn't have many perks, other than the twenty- percent discount. And that's if I didn't lose my job. I was missing a lot of hours, because I was too sick to stay at a cash register. And the bottom line was that we didn't have the Sid-and–Nancy-Sex Pistols-murder-suicide kind of love that would see us through the hard times.

I'd made peace with the fact that I was having this child. What I was going to do with the little darling once it arrived was still up in the air.

Option two was that my mom offered to raise my baby as her own. She and Loren would never tell. I would get to see my progeny every day if I wanted or once a week. Whatever was in my comfort zone.

Or, option three, they could take the baby until I got on my feet. Once I made some real decisions about the direction of my life, then I could have my baby back.

As if we were talking about a goldfish.

The fourth option was finding a family that really wanted a baby—magically locating a family that couldn't have children, who needed an infant 'someone' to make their family whole.

After the distasteful appointment with the lady with the baby vacuum, that option was so out.

I truly considered having my mom raise my baby. But once I could see past my own selfish nose, I realized that it would be an incredible strain on a newly married couple, who were just about finished raising their combined teenagers.

What right did I have to foist my hormonal bad judgment on them?

And how could I live through each day, seeing my mom and step dad shower 'their' baby with love, and not feel jealousy or remorse or guilt? I was already drowning in unfamiliar emotion, I couldn't add that too and stay sane.

But I knew in my heart that I couldn't raise a child on my own. I couldn't. I didn't even know how to boil an egg.

Every dream I'd had for my future was forgotten, and my world now revolved around my burgeoning belly, my knowledge of the 'best' public bathrooms for hurling privacy, and my constant sense of confusion and doubt and angst.

Was I hungry? Tired? Nauseous? Was the baby going to be okay? Would he/she forgive me for not wanting him/her in the beginning? I would just have to love it enough that any doubts would be lost forever.

I didn't have health insurance, but I made an appointment with my mom's doctor, and he saw me free of charge. He prescribed prenatal vitamins, rest, and lots of milk.

No smoking, no coffee.

No problem.

He didn't understand why my morning sickness hadn't gone away, but chalked it up to 'one of those things.'

The baby grew, and I stayed healthy—even without the nauseating prenatal vitamins. Sleeping wasn't an issue. I liked it a lot. Not only was I exhausted, but I didn't have to make a decision or go over my self-absorbed life with a fine-tooth comb when I was snoozing. It's just that I wasn't ever tired at *night.*

Dark would fall and I'd wake up for a few hours just as my family was going to bed. I distracted myself with the occasional show—a collection of punk bands that got together wherever they could rent a place to play. I couldn't drink or mosh, but I could still listen to the angry slash of bass or the furious thump of drums. The music often echoed what I felt inside, and I'd scream the lyrics until my throat hurt.

As I got further along in my pregnancy, I noticed that my baby loved the music too, and he or she was much more active at night.

We were nocturnal. That was sort of a bond, right?

I was terrified of losing my friends. Of being replaced in the scene by younger, non-pregnant girls, who could dance and flirt and wear midriff-baring tanks.

When nasty gossip and rumors ran through our little scene like wild fire, I found out who my real friends were. I was amazed that I had so many.

By the time I was five-months pregnant, Ricky still hadn't officially moved over from Seattle. He'd been to see me a few times, and I was cautiously hopeful that we might stay together. He talked marriage, or at least about moving in together.

Even in my most desperate moments, I never allowed myself to believe that Ricky was 'the one.' But he cared for me, and I didn't want to go through this scary time all alone.

My mom's wedding helped take some of the intense focus off my crazy life. She still wanted me to be a part of the wedding party, even though I was quite obviously pregnant.

She made our dresses herself, so that we could all have similar styles. My stepsister and I were in purple, and she wore yellow. By this time, I could see and understand why my mom loved my stepdad so much. Loren was so kind, so cool, and so much in love with her.

I remember a particular picture of us all. Me, my stepsister, my brother—before his giant growth spurt—my uncle Jim, Mom and Loren. We were a patched together family in lavender, yellow and gray. Family.

I never got the sense that any of them were judging me. They accepted and loved me, no matter what. They gave me the strength to do what was right for me.

Looking back, I must have been isolated from most of the gossip, although I was hyperaware that people were noticing my weight gain. We weren't yelling the news of my upcoming baby from the rooftops, so at the wedding I think some people thought I was just helping myself to too many Twinkies and Black Label beers. This was actually preferable to the finger pointing and behind the hand whispers, as other people refused to meet my gaze.

My mom and Loren both fiercely defended my decision, and my right to choose my future. Witnessing their wedding vows, and seeing the love between Loren and Mom as they held each other's hands, cemented in my head what a marriage *should* be.

Yeah, it took Mom three times before she found it. But she'd found it—finally. I didn't want to make any more bad decisions just because I was afraid of being alone. Well, afraid of being a single parent.

Later, I told Ricky that I wouldn't marry him…I liked him—he was really cute—but I didn't love him enough for forever. I thanked him for the offer, but let him off the hook.

He told me that I was the coolest girl in the world, and that he still wanted to be with me. He would wait, or so he said. He'd come to Spokane to live and be in my life. In the baby's life. I promised that whatever happened, he would be a part of it, and I even helped him find a place to stay once he moved from Seattle.

I seesawed with hormones and emotions, and I just couldn't figure out what I needed to do. I lacked focus.

My brain churned in slow motion, and I couldn't fix it.

Tired, sick and depressed—that was me. I had stretch marks. I couldn't fit into any of my clothes, not even my big shirts. My aunt loaned me some of my uncle's.

The Good, the Bad, and the Ugly

I had to shop in the maternity section, while my friends were wearing skinny jeans and getting tattooed.

But I had awesome friends, and I even made an unexpected friend, one who really saw me through some dark times. My girlfriends were great, but Dan talked me through a lot of crap. He was there when life threatened to pull me under.

Until I got too big, he took me riding around Spokane on the back of his scooter. He was a guitarist in one of my very favorite local punk bands, and even though he had a reputation as a loner, we became close friends.

For him, I was a 'safe' girl to talk to. I didn't want to be in his bed, for one thing. I had a sort of boyfriend, and I was super pregnant. Even at five months, you could tell that I wasn't just hiding a few pounds.

It became a familiar joke when we'd go out to eat that I needed to stop binging and purging.

I didn't want anything other than his friendship, and I think he felt the same way. Things might have changed, because he did ask me to go to Maine with him. He said we'd walk on the beach, look at lighthouses and collect sea shells. We'd run away. As soon as the baby was born...

To a broken girl from Spokane, that idea totally rocked. But I didn't go.

Dan was a sanity saver, especially once Ricky finally moved from Seattle and found his own place in the scene. Because he was FROM Seattle, and because he was very, very cute, he had an immediate herd of groupies.

I couldn't compete with them on any level. And to be honest, since I'd already told him I wasn't interested in forever, just for now, I wasn't sure that I had any right to be the center of his attention.

The Good, the Bad, and the Ugly

It hurt like hell when I found him drunk and making out with my good friend's sister. They were in the middle of the street, and they had their arms wrapped around each other's very slim waists.

Talk about bad days.

We were over after that, although I think we did try once or twice more before we decided to be just friends.

Eventually, it got to the point where we weren't even that.

With all of the emotional garbage I was already going through, I couldn't handle his kind of being in my life.

Dashed hope is a hard thing to accept. There'd been a tiny part of me that had wished for a happy ever after, where Ricky would move to Spokane, get a job, and keep his pants on. He'd prove that he loved only me and our baby, and eventually we'd be a family.

It was clear that wasn't going to happen.

Despite his intentions, I was going to be a single parent.

On welfare.

I felt so hopeless and trapped. What could I do?

I wanted to write, but dreams don't make money. Hard work makes money. In three months, I'd be a florist. I'd get to work long hours over the holidays and every weekend. Woo hoo! Not.

My mom would end up babysitting, and it wasn't her responsibility to take care of my child.

The image of the five-hundred-pound me, living a life of drudgery, wouldn't go away, What if I ended up on Jerry Springer? What if I raised a kid who would grow up miserable in the welfare system, and he or she would rebel by snorting a little coke? Maybe he or she would then turn into a crackhead, or do tricks for heroin…and it would be all my fault.

Considering my family history, it could happen. Ricky's gene pool wasn't any better.

I was so scared. Worse, I was struck by the cloudiness of my future. I couldn't see it, so I couldn't plan for it. Not in any way that had a happy ending.

And then came the first time I saw my baby's foot against my belly.

I'd felt the occasional mysterious movement, but I was the queen of cracked ribs from hurling. The baby was a gymnast in the womb, going round and round. Yet this first clear imprint of my child pressing its heel against my skin made me totally and completely freak out.

Breathless, I waited for it to happen again.

I was in no way prepared for the tidal wave of love that consumed me. I was going to have this baby. A real human being, with needs, wants and desires.

Love.

Doubt.

My baby should have a stable home, with parents who loved him and could send him to the best schools and get him to college and maybe go on yearly family vacations.

Floored, stunned, frozen…I was loaded down with uncertainty and guilt and expectation. How could I fail at this? *How could I not?*

Another wave of love—the purest, most unconditional love I'd ever known—sent me over the edge. I cried and cried, because I knew I had to somehow make it right.

The Good, the Bad, and the Ugly

But how?

My mom and I got into a big fight about what I was going to do, as if she could tell me. As if she were somehow deliberately hiding the answers from me.

My attitude, combined with all the emotional upheaval, was horrible. When she called one afternoon to tell me she'd found an ad for a lawyer who did private adoptions, and that I should at least consider it, I lost it.

My first reaction was fury—she'd zeroed in on my secret fear, that I couldn't be a good parent. Later she explained that she was trying to show me that she understood my worry that loving the baby was not enough—the child needed to be cared for too. She'd also hit on my secret desire—*to not be a parent at all.*

Rhonda Pollero

CHAPTER FOUR

Hello, Good-Bye, and Good Luck

Playing Charades: How to Ease Your Way into Parenthood Without Getting Your Feelings Hurt.

I hid the sting of being rejected, showered and fell into my big, comfy, wonderful bed. I think I was asleep before my head hit the pillow. As is my habit, I rose early the next morning. Earlier than usual, thanks to the pain in my jaw. It was a good thing, because for the first time in forever, I had good coffee with cream and enjoyed the silence and lack of companionship. I watched the sunrise as I sat on the porch, and then read several articles I'd pulled from the Internet regarding bonding issues with adopted children.

Even though many of the articles described terrible outcomes, just reading academic essays and anecdotal stories from adoptive parents made me feel better. I was buoyed; sure I could—and would—eventually get my daughter to trust me.

Katie had gone to sleep before seven. It was thirteen hours later, and I didn't hear a peep from her room. Good, I was glad she was catching up on her sleep. I dressed and left my house at 8:50 to kept my dentist appointment. It took him a little over an hour, but the abscess was taken care of, and stage one of the root canal was complete. I returned home to find Bob still sleeping, so I listened intently. Still no sounds of stirring from Katie's bedroom.

By eleven, I began to worry, so I went up to check on her. She was wide awake and sitting on the edge of the bed, sneakered feet dangling. I reached my hand out to her, but she didn't budge. I thought about calling Bob in as reinforcement, but all the expert literature I'd been reading said that wasn't the best approach. So, I walked over and picked her up. Amazingly, she didn't struggle, wiggle, spit or bite. Instead, she wound her tiny arms around my neck and let me carry her downstairs to the kitchen.

I talked incessantly, describing everything I was doing as I made her oatmeal and scrambled eggs. She mutely looked on with hooded, distrustful eyes, as I cooked and presented her with breakfast. The one thing she never needed was encouragement to eat. So long as the temperature and texture were to her liking, she would gorge herself.

Step two was getting her dressed. I opened the closet and asked, "Which one?" Then went outfit by outfit, talking and pointing…green pants, green shirt, sundress with watermelon, etc. After the inventory, I touched each one, then nodded and shook my head while saying 'yes' and 'no' in phonetic Russian. When that didn't elicit a response, I physically took each outfit down and held them against her, playing a second round of English/Russian charades.

It took some time, but I finally got a 'Da' on a denim sundress with daisies embroidered around the hem.

"Da, yes," I said, relating the Russian response with its English equivalent. And so it began. Thanks to the pocket guide that provided English-to-Russian and Russian-to-English, everything I said was in simple, one- or two-word sentences in both languages.

"*Papa schpot*, Daddy sleeping. *Pah-kah, machine-a.* Go bye-bye in the car." Most of my attempts at communication included charades and/or examples.

Katie still preferred Bob and enjoyed her weekend with him. I got the short end of that stick, because he'd ask me to do the translation, and then repeat it to her and, in no time, Katie was saying a few things in both Russian and English. We were making progress.

Then Monday morning came, and Bob had to go to work. "*Pah-kuh, Papa.* Bye-bye Daddy," brought tears and a full-out fit. I had to deadbolt the door to keep her from running after him. Even though I repeated over and over again that Daddy would come back, it took an hour to calm her down. That was repeated every morning for a week and when Daddy did come home, she squealed with delight.

I, on the other hand, could go out without Katie so much as a glancing in my direction. I'd be lying if I didn't say a part of me was feeling resentful. I was spending hours every day working on building her vocabulary and introducing her to her new world. Not as easy as it sounds. The child had never felt grass beneath her feet. She'd never seen a hose or a sprinkler or television or, well, anything. She also had some orphanage habits—hoarding was a big thing. Almost anything she was given or found, she'd tuck behind her back or sit on it, fearful of having anything taken away from her.

She still ate to excess, and I had to be careful to portion her food accordingly. But the hardest activities that first week were taking her to the pediatrician and the dentist. Luckily, my pediatrician spoke Russian. Unfortunately, all the Russian in the world didn't seem to calm her when she figured out she had to have immunizations. It took three nurses and me to hold her down for each shot.

The dentist was another problem. He finally ended up

having to use nitrous oxide, just so the years of plaque buildup could be scraped from her teeth.

I was the one taking her to all these appointments, so it didn't exactly help our mother-daughter bonding. Other responsibilities in those early days included: applying for her Social Security number, starting the citizenship process, and readopting her in Maryland. Yes, that last one sounds stupid, because, well, it is. But my State required that we file for a decree of adoption, so it was back to the land of the apositiled for me.

The Social Security thing was an adventure. I went into the building in Glen Burnie, Maryland, glanced at the directory and took the elevator to the second floor. I entered a room crowded with women and children and was pretty stunned to see so many people with adopted children doing the same thing I was doing. Yet again, I took a number and a seat. Katie played with other children, while I waited and waited and waited. After two hours, I was finally called to the counter. It was only then that I discovered I'd gone to the wrong room. I was in the WIC application room. Social Security card applications were handled in the office one floor up. Note to prospective adoptive parents: read for comprehension.

On the way home from the Social Security office, I decided to stop at the grocery store. It was the first time I'd taken Katie into a store, and to say it was a fiasco doesn't begin to describe the chaos she caused. As a child reared in an orphanage, she thought everything was communal and up for grabs. She refused to sit in the cart, so I had to hold her wrist as I steered the one-wheel-doesn't-work cart up and down the aisles. Any time I stopped to get an item, Katie would grab something and tear it open before I could wrestle it from her hands. Embarrassed, I put all the items she destroyed in my cart, including the two bottles of witch hazel, and abandoned the notion of shopping with her in tow. As we waited to check out, she opened seven candy bars and yanked a hair clip out of another child's hair. I was apologizing, explaining and sympathizing, since Katie had taken a small hunk of the kid's hair along with the clip. Other kid's mommy was not pleased.

Small moments of humiliation aside, my relationship with Katie wasn't exactly improving. She still preferred Bob to me and, at least once a week, she was still spitting in my face. I read in one of the articles that the spitting thing was common. There were serious and unpleasant consequences if a child put their hands on another child in the orphanage. Spitting was their way around that rule.

About a month after Katie came home, the tide turned. I wish I could say it was because I'd been her teacher, her disciplinarian, her driver, and seen to her every need. None of that mattered. Life in our house changed when Katie bit Bob hard enough to break the skin. She'd been doing that to me for weeks, but this was his first taste of Katie's wrath. His disapproval and rather swift reaction to the bite caught her off guard. Daddy, who until then was all fun and games, plopped her fanny on the naughty step and sternly chastised her. It was the first time he'd spoken to her harshly, and as tears spilled down her cheeks, she cried out, "Momma!"

As thrilled as I was that she finally wanted me, I didn't interfere. Instead, I told Bob to let me be the one to get her from the naughty spot after her three minutes of penance. When I did, she hugged me for the first time. Not the reluctant, loose hold, but a tight squeeze that nearly broke my hyoid bone.

I dried her tears and in Russian-English, I told her biting was wrong and she had to tell her daddy that she was sorry. At first she refused, but when she realized we were headed back to the naughty step, she quickly said, "Sorry, Daddy."

From that day on, we began to build the bond I'd almost dismissed as a flight of fancy. It wasn't instantaneous, and we suffered a few setbacks along the way. Like a sponge, she learned English and gradually the Russian-English charades became a thing of the past. By November, she spoke like a native.

My hurt feelings healed and now that we were conversing, I was really getting to know her as a person. One thing became clear. She was lonely. Accustomed to the company of 153 other children, she missed having little friends and structured play. To solve that problem, we put her in a half-day program, five days a week, at The Goddard School. She not only enjoyed it, she thrived. Every day she would come home with new words, experiences and an eagerness to share her adventures.

Her assimilation into her new world was fast and nothing short of amazing. By Christmas, her vocabulary even included slang. Most importantly, she was happy.

Traci Hall

CHAPTER FOUR

Hello, Good-Bye, and Good Luck

Picking Parents for Forever

I called my mom a name for the one and only time in my life. Angry and scared, I was like a cornered, rabid raccoon. And yet…

Once I'd calmed down, and once she'd calmed down, we talked about the ad she'd seen. About what it could mean.

This wasn't a state-run facility for adoption; this was a respected lawyer's office. One of their specialties was private adoption.

What could it hurt? I could go in and talk to them at least. Maybe ask some questions. *If* I felt comfortable.

The minute somebody asked me to watch a little film, we were outta there!

As I remember, the offices were nice, homey, and much more welcoming than the government office for adoption, which had been sterile and cold.

Framed certificates hung on the papered walls, and a discreet notebook lay on top of Mrs. J's polished, cherry wood desk.

We shook hands, and she didn't look at me like I was moron, which was a great start. She treated me with respect and dignity, as if my opinion on where I thought my baby should live deserved to be heard.

The state-run facility could learn a lesson from the lawyer's office...

Once we finished the introductions, she talked about what services she provided. She handled private adoptions between searching families and potential birth mothers. The nominal fee—I think it was three-hundred dollars—would be paid by the adopting family. Her families included doctors and lawyers, as well as engineers and teachers.

I admit that I was blown away by the fact that my baby could have doctors for parents. My child could be sent to private school, summer camp—whatever he or she wanted, they could possibly have.

And a couple who wanted a baby so bad they were willing to hire a lawyer, well...I patted my stomach, which was growing by the hour. My child would be the lucky recipient of their prosperity.

There was a bubble of hope in my heart that I was afraid might burst before I could really appreciate it. Squishing it down, I listened closely as she explained that private adoptions had more benefits for the birth mother than standard adoption agencies, because I could choose who my child went to.

That blew me away.

I could handpick my baby's new parents?

Oh my God.

I could not only have an opinion, I had the power to decide. I remember my leg jiggling, I was so nervous. I asked, "I can pick? How do I do that? Where would I start?"

The lawyer pushed the notebook across her desk to me. "Open it."

Fingers trembling, I did. Inside the notebook were about half a dozen pictures of parents who were all desperately searching for another human being to add to their lives.

Two of the families had other children already.

She pointed to each picture as I turned the pages, explaining a little about who each family was. "These two are both doctors, but she wants to stay home and raise a family. She can't get pregnant, and they really want a child."

I stared at the couple in the photo who, outwardly, had everything. Money, looks, careers…but the one thing that they really wanted—a baby—had been denied.

I could help them achieve their dream for a family.

Again, the possibilities for my baby were endless.

But…I shifted in my seat as a tiny foot jammed under my rib. I was getting more and more attached to the baby inside me every day.

I told myself that things would work out somehow for the next eighteen years, and we'd be fine. Me and my baby living off of Gov'ment Cheese in subsidized housing.

Yuck.

I was currently eligible for welfare, but I didn't want it. For the moment, I had food and shelter and my mom's doctor to see me through.

Signing up for government help seemed so final. Food stamps would be an admission into a trapped life that I didn't want to live. I had a definite bias about accepting help. I was wary of getting sucked into a welfare life and never getting off.

Hello, Good-Bye, and Good Luck

I had two hands, and I wasn't afraid to sweat. My mom worked two jobs, sometimes three, to make ends meet. My grandmothers are both very strong women, who didn't shy away from doing whatever it took to get the job done.

Welfare seemed like charity—but the reality was that I needed clothes that fit, and my job at Newberry's wasn't working out because I'd been so sick.

As I sat in the chair, uncomfortable at owning up to yet another character flaw, I let the realization that I wasn't sold on the idea of being a mother seep in a bit more.

I was eighteen and pregnant, but not mom material. That doctor woman in the pictures could stay home all day and happily dedicate herself to bottle feeding and diaper changing.

I couldn't do that—more so—*I didn't want to do that.*

Choosing a family, the best family, would allow me a chance to do something good.

I'd made a mistake, but I accepted it and the consequences. What if… what if I didn't have to be a mom yet? I could give birth, and give my baby to a family that would treat my child like precious gold.

I said, "The only thing that would make this easier would be knowing that I could get a few pictures or something. You know, just every once in a while."

The lawyer smiled. "You're talking about open adoption. Some of the families have already expressed an interest in that."

"What's open adoption?" My shoulders tensed defensively as I waited for her answer. So far I liked the idea of a private adoption—now that I knew it was possible, I didn't want something else.

"That means there are less rules. You make them up between the two of you."

Sighing with relief, I thought about all of the forms in triplicate that the other adoption lady had said I'd need to sign. Like I was signing everything away with no benefit. Anyway, I liked the idea of not having so many rules.

"Does that mean that someday the baby could know me?"

She nodded, and I exchanged a glance with my mom.

"It would be totally cool with me, if they knew my name and stuff."

"The great thing about open adoption is that there is a lot of communication, or a little communication, depending on what you and the baby's adoptive family would decide."

"It doesn't have to be a secret?" I was intrigued by this concept. Somehow this became very important to me. Being upfront about everything held huge appeal. I didn't want to feel ashamed of my choice to give my baby up for adoption, and I reveled in that first little glimmer of excitement. This could be a way to have it all. But I wasn't ready to give in completely yet.

Better to read the fine print before signing on the dotted line, right?

"Nope. No secrets…well," she quickly amended, "we don't recommend that you know where the adoptive family lives exactly, or vice versa. This style of adoption is still so new that we're learning too. My job is to help facilitate the agreement, but it can be tailored so that both parties are comfortable."

This sounded good—great, actually—but I wanted things spelled out. "I can tell them that I want pictures every Christmas? Every birthday?" My heart hammered and the baby kicked, probably protesting at the surge of adrenalin.

She smiled. "We recommend getting a post office box for the first year so that any correspondence between you can be private. After that, you renegotiate, and if you need my help, I'll do it." She tapped her fingers against the desktop. "You might not think so now, but in five years, you could change your mind about how much or how little interaction you'd like. The same is true for the adoptive family. You'll have to respect their wishes, just as they should respect yours."

I exchanged a look with my mom. This sounded too good to be true. The woman at the adoption center had been horrible and very adamant that meeting the adoptive parents was harmful.

That I had to give up my baby and never look back, for both of our sakes.

My mom was nodding, and I remember thinking that this just might be an answer to a prayer I hadn't realized I'd uttered.

By the time we left the lawyer's office, I was feeling curiously optimistic. We didn't make an immediate decision, but we spent the next few days going over the pros and cons of private versus open adoption.

Keeping and raising this baby on my own settled to the back of my mind.

There was no information on open adoption at the time. Adoptions were government run, and hushed up as another dirty secret—the part that came after doing 'you know what' to get pregnant in the first place. I wasn't the kind to hide away, even if I had made a serious error in judgment.

I didn't feel capable of being a good mom, let alone the kind of mom my baby deserved to have, but I still wanted what was best for him or her.

Making me feel ashamed didn't help spur me toward a

decision. I already knew what I'd done 'wrong.' I did a lot of soul searching. Dug down into all of my deep, dark psyche corners and prodded until I was raw.

Having a less than perfect childhood didn't give me the right to be a bad mom. I was always certain that my mom loved me, even though we'd just recently mended a relationship that had fragmented during tough times.

She was proof that maternal love lasted through thick and thin. But love didn't put food on the table, or a roof over anybody's head. I could love this baby, this innocent infant, best by finding a home where he or she would be cherished.

If and when my baby wanted to contact me, open adoption would allow my child to know exactly where I was at, and find me. It gave me the option of changing my mind, too. I wouldn't want my baby to meet me if I turned into a serial killer or something.

I could explain, no matter how much it hurt, about why I'd done what I had. I'd answer any questions he or she would have. Openly and honestly.

This was an opportunity that I hadn't seen coming, and I jumped at it as if it were a life preserver and I was drowning.

Considering I was a hormonal teenager who had been on an emotional seesaw for six and a half months, that analogy fit.

When I finally made the decision to go back to the lawyer's office and try for an open adoption, a huge weight lifted off my heart. I could do the right thing—the best thing—for this baby without putting either of us at risk.

Within seconds, my ever-active brain pointed out that my worries were far from over. If anything, they'd escalated. I now had the sole responsibility of choosing my baby's parents.

What if I accidentally picked a family of axe murderers?

When my mom and I went in to officially sign with Mrs. J., I had a list of things that I thought were important to know before I made my selection. Love, money, family support. Vacations were a big priority. No jail birds. No arrest records.

I went back to the photo of the two doctors. The wife wanted to stay home and be a full-time mom. I had this ridiculous image in my head of her wearing an apron and baking cookies.

She'd probably puree homemade baby food.

I measured water to boil pasta.

I handed my list to Mrs. J., who assured me that all of her clients had passed a rigorous background check. Not a single pedophile among them. I still worried. This was forever.

My mom stayed with me, and we set up interviews with different couples. Not all of them were comfortable with open adoption, and some decided that they would only be interested if it was private.

I was stuck on the open and honest thing, though. It's amazing how things fell into place.

I got in touch with Ricky, letting him know what was happening, as I'd promised I would. He had to sign off as daddy, anyway. Rumor had it that he'd already gotten another girl in our scene pregnant.

He promised me it wasn't true.

I believed him when he said he wanted to try again. He even went to two interviews with me before getting physically ill and bagging out.

He wasn't a lot of help and, in the end, I chose the family I wanted based on intuition and a gut instinct.

Hello, Good-Bye, and Good Luck

I spent a lot of time talking to my tummy. Whispering that I loved him or her, and that I would do my best to find a family that was practically perfect.

Perfect would be too boring.

My baby was very active and had a tendency to curl up against a nerve in my spine—adding pain to my nausea.

Now that I knew I was going to search for the right parents—and only the right parents—I didn't mind the aches at all.

Rhonda Pollero

CHAPTER FIVE
Door Half Closed

Are You My Mother?
What to Tell You and When.

I can't count the number of people who praise us for 'saving' Katie from the orphanage. The truth is, she saved us. Having Katie in our lives helped us heal from the devastation of losing Kyle. Raising her has forced us to move on, past the grief.

We did—and do—still mourn for our son. We always will. You don't get over the death of your child and time does not heal all wounds. At best, it just gets different. Having Katie reminded us that the best way to honor our son's memory was to go on living.

But we had a new issue. How to help Katie understand that she was adopted and what adoption means. There's no handbook on this issue. It's a play-it-by-ear kind of thing. Obviously, we had to use the word so she'd be comfortable with it. It wasn't a topic we could avoid. It wasn't like we could lie and say, "You were an ugly baby, so we didn't take any pictures of you until you were three." And she had some memories of Russia. They were jumbled and blurry and probably influenced by us telling her stories, but that wasn't the problem. The problem was how to be honest without being *completely* honest.

At three, adoption is just a word. When asked, we explained that it meant that she was our daughter in every way that mattered, but it had taken us time to find her in Russia. At four, she asked how she ended up in Russia, since her friend's mother was pregnant and the new baby would be born here, not in Russia. We explained that sometimes the person who gives birth to a baby isn't the person who is supposed to raise that baby. Babies are cute, so it takes a brave and kind person to give up the baby to make sure the baby ends up with her forever family. By the time she was five or six, Katie finally asked me what a birth mother was. I told her and then explained that her birth mother was in Russia and, since Russia had food shortages and other things that make it hard to raise a child, her birth mother had decided to give her up so she'd go to another family and never be hungry or cold.

That was the last time she asked me anything about adoption or birth mothers. Secretly, I'm thrilled. But I know it's only a matter of time before she asks the really hard questions, and I'm still not sure how I'll deal with them. The family history we were given is not pleasant nor does it paint her birth family in a particularly positive light. I worry about how she'll react to the truth. I feel as if I'm walking a tightrope. She deserves to know everything I know; it's just a matter of timing. She has to reach a certain level of maturity to be able to understand things like alcoholism, questionable paternity, fetal alcohol syndrome, abandonment, abuse and incarceration.

Hopefully, we've provided her with enough stability so that when she does have all the pieces, she'll be able to handle reading the documents describing those first three years of her life.

Traci Hall

CHAPTER FIVE

Door Half Closed

From a Distance—I'm Your Mom,
But Not Your Mom

The 'professionals' all said that when giving a child up for adoption, the birth mom should get a pet.

I brought home a darling gray-and-white kitten that we named Pseudo. With my characteristic bluntness, I told the kitten that she was just a stand in for the real thing, but she didn't seem to mind.

She slept on my mountain of a tummy and lightly swatted at the moving parts. Her deep purr was a comfort against the aches and overall ickiness.

Most women go through pregnancy with the incentive that they will have something wonderful at the end of it. A healthy baby. The newest addition to a family.

I was going through my very odd pregnancy not knowing what would happen. Stress can make you crazy. Lucky for me, I had excellent support.

I was lucky to have friends who didn't mind playing the what-if game.

Carrie: What if it's a girl?

Michelle: Could be a boy.

Susie: It would be funny if it was twins.

Me: Shut up already! That would so *not* be funny.

Carrie: You could change your mind.

Me: If I find the right parents, I won't change my mind. I won't have to go on welfare, or be a single mom who does nothing but chain smoke (as I wave away C's cigarette) and complain.

Michelle: Once you do this, you can't change your mind.

Me: Do you really think I'd be a good mom? Come on! I don't even know how to do laundry. I don't have a car, and now I don't even have a job. What am I gonna do—be a florist? They don't make squat.

Susie: We could help.

Me: That's sweet. But this is a baby, not a doll. I hated dolls. Decapitated all of my Barbies. You think I'd be safe around a real baby? What if he or she got lost in the park? (Real worry overrides the joking, and I can't breathe for a second—the realization that there is so much that I can't control is deafening)

Dan: What do they do with the placenta?

Susie: I hear they sell placenta shampoo—it's supposed to be really good for your hair.

Me: That's sick. You both are sick. (I take a bite of the hot fudge brownie that is oozing vanilla ice cream) Besides, I can't think about the actual *having* the baby part.

Dan: It's gonna hurt.

Michelle: You can have drugs…that shot thing they put in your back.

Carrie: My sister had it…it's an epidermis.

Michelle: (sighing) Epidural.

Susie: A needle in your back? Ouch!

Me: I am not getting a shot in my spine. There's a risk of getting paralyzed. No way.

Dan: (smirking) You're going to do it with no drugs? You're insane.

Me: A woman can't get paralyzed birthing a child naturally.

Dan: I want to see the placenta.

Me: Get over the placenta! What if he—

Susie: Or she!

Carrie: It'll be a boy.

Me: What if he or she grows up and hates me for giving him away? That could really happen.

Moment of silence as we all stare at the dark brown goo on the plate.

Michelle: She—

Dan: He.

Susie: Won't hate you.

Carrie: He won't.

Me: I don't know. I guess I'll just have to live with it. I mean, I hope I can explain someday. (Rubbing my belly like I'm Buddha, I send loving thoughts—a prayer against hate.)

Dan: Diddly Squat's in town next weekend. Wanna go?

Me: Yeah. Let's ask Bonnie, too.

Carrie: I am not going to listen to that crappy music. I have to work, anyway.

Susie: I'm in!

Michelle: Me too.

Me: Ow! (Patting tummy where a foot is pressing out.)

Dan: What if you swallowed an alien?

When my friends weren't cheering me up, I slept. I finished Floral Design and Business Management. I spent so much time wondering if my decision was the right one that I barely knew my own name anymore. I'd already screwed up in spades, so I didn't necessarily trust my judgment.

There were legal issues—like Ricky and I both had to sign papers at the lawyer's office. Ricky had to officially give up his parental rights.

I think it hit him hard, the realization of what was happening. He really tried to care—he did. But he was seventeen, just about eighteen, and he'd gotten me pregnant during a one-night deal. We'd tried hard to make it more than that, but it wasn't working.

Talk about needing a reality check. I felt bad for him, and it was easier to fall into a strange relationship than it should have been.

He'd call me, drunk, and apologize for who knows what sins. I'd only want him when he was gone, and I was feeling alone and sorry for myself.

It wasn't until he got Mara pregnant that the fog cleared. He wasn't going to grow up—and how could I expect him to?

Yeah, he partied. Until I'd gotten pregnant, so had I. It was a blast to hang out until the early hours of the morning, if we had a place to crash or until the last bus run, if we didn't.

Live music was in my blood—my dad was a musician—and something about the crash of sound connected me to myself.

I needed to pour myself into something else, and it turned out to be writing. I wrote angst-ridden poetry that was so dark and melodramatic, I tossed it a few years later.

I wrote lyrics and promises. I slept a lot, and dreamed of what my life might turn out to be like.

Giving up my baby meant that I had something to prove.

I couldn't be a loser forever. This was a chance for my child, and a chance for me.

If I stayed in Spokane, with the same people and the same lack of expectations, I would always be trapped with cuffs of my own making.

I owed it to myself, and my baby, to be better than I was. I couldn't fall back into the same old crap. If I were a florist, then I'd create masterpieces that would win blue ribbons. Or if I were a writer, I'd be up for every award—including the Pulitzer! I couldn't let myself get moved along on the tide of mediocrity.

I remember having way too much time to think. That can be a dangerous thing. The closer I got to my due date, the higher my self-expectations rose. I knew that I'd have to be so perfectly deserving of my child that nothing less than the Presidency would do. Well, maybe being a brain surgeon. Saint Traci had a nice ring to it.

I wanted so badly to make something good out of something traumatic. Even though the event was of my own making, I was eighteen and undergoing the equivalent of ten-years-maturing experience crammed into a few months.

Nobody should have to pull themselves apart like that unless they're going into the priesthood. The trick was to try and put myself back together again in a way that I could live with. I had to create self-respect so that I could stick to the life changes I'd already put in motion.

There wasn't anything easy about any of the decisions that I'd made so far, and there wasn't anything easy about the stuff coming up in my life either.

Just one glaring example was the changes in my body. I had stretch marks along my tummy that would never go away, and they would require an explanation to anybody who saw them. I wasn't thinking of taking up a career in pole dancing, so chances were that whoever was that close would be someone I trusted. But still...

Each time I'd tell my story, I would be judged. At eighteen, I should have known better than to have unprotected sex. I got it. Loud and clear.

I would have to have the strength to know that I'd made the right choice, no matter what other people might think about me and/or my morals.

That is a lot to ask of an eighteen, almost nineteen-year-old ex-party girl.

I think all of that self-examination was necessary in order for me to give my baby to a family who could nurture and provide for him better than I could.

But there were days when I hated myself and everybody around me. It was easy to blame fate or God. Unfortunately, I was too pragmatic to ever blame anybody other than myself for long.

The times when I knew that life would be okay were few and far between, but they happened.

Meeting the parents—the 'ones'—was one of those days.

Originally, I had picked the two doctors as the perfect family. They had the shiny veneer of success in their bright smiles. I've never really been comfortable with perfection, though, and so I'd hesitated before agreeing to sign with them.

When they got a chance to adopt a little girl from China, they went ahead with it.

They said they were still interested in taking my baby too, but it just didn't feel right to me. Besides, they hadn't been excited about the open adoption.

Not that I could blame them. Legally, the rights were all in my favor, and I could pull out of our agreement at any time.

Adoptive parents have to put a lot of faith in the birth mother—they go into the process knowing that the plan to adopt could change at any moment.

Looking back, it took a lot of courage for any of these prospective parents to even try open adoption.

It was new at the time, and risky. They could emotionally and financially invest in an empty promise.

The perks were a chance at a faster turnaround. The State remains mired within its own red tape, and it can take years before a couple's name might come up as being eligible parents.

Another plus was that they could interview me, too. They could meet me and see if I had most of my teeth, that sort of thing. Normally, that doesn't happen in an adoption situation.

This can also be placed in the risk column—some people preferred the anonymity of never meeting. It's safe. However, I was on a quest for a family that would be the best fit for my baby, and what better way than to meet face to face?

I wasn't comfortable with having my baby be an "add

on" to the doctor's family. I understand her desperation to be a mother better now than I did then, but I remember clearly the relief I felt at being able to—guilt free—part ways.

When the lawyer called with a new prospective family, I was kind of depressed. Maybe I'd been wrong to think that adoption was the path to take—I couldn't give my baby to parents I didn't connect with.

I wanted my child to grow up happy, healthy, and loved.

I wanted him or her to have chocolate cookie smiles and be able to finger paint in the mud without getting yelled at for making a mess.

I admit to being (throat clearing) moody. It's amazing my mom didn't ship me off to some deserted island or put me in a padded room until it was all over.

Turning nineteen had me in a tailspin. No parties, no fun, no perfect parents for my unborn child.

Other people were having a good time—going to Seattle, seeing the Violent Femmes in concert, stuff I'd do if I could. But I couldn't, and it was my own fault.

Poor, poor me.

I don't think I was being very cool about this new family, but I went, knowing I couldn't leave any possibility unchecked.

And then I found them.

Fate, God, a miracle no matter what you call it, put THE family in my path.

I saw their picture and fell head over heels—I was positive that they were IT. The mom had dark wavy hair, a pretty smile, and she had her hand on the shoulder of a dark haired little boy with sparkling eyes. Next to her was a man with dark hair and a grin.

Door Half Closed

They looked like fun.

They reminded me of my aunt and uncle, who were the only solidly married, happy, still-together couple in my family. My aunt could make chocolate chip pancakes with teddy bear ears, and she and my uncle would welcome anyone into their home and share a meal. They boated, they hiked and they laughed. They had friends who were as close as family, which made things even more chaotic. My brother and I were always included in the fun. We were wanted. We were a part of something.

That something, that magical something, jumped out of the photo.

"Who are they?"

"It's a funny story, actually," Mrs. J. said.

I looked at my mom and smiled, my bad mood evaporating like a dark cloud against the sun. "They remind me of Aunt Vicki and Uncle Paul."

I couldn't give a higher compliment than that. "How did you find them?" *Where had they been hiding?*

They were *my* idea of perfection. They weren't millionaires, and they weren't perfectly made up—they were real, and they looked *happy.*

My baby could fit in that picture, right next to the little boy with the wavy hair and shy smile.

"Why do they need to adopt?" I couldn't stop staring at the photo. "Can't she have any more kids?" The smiling lady looked like she could be a mom to ten kids without batting an eye.

"There's a health concern, I think," Mrs. J. said with a shrug. "And it just so happens that this couple's name came to us through an unusual source—a friend of a friend kind of situation."

She didn't elaborate, and I didn't pry. I was too busy imagining my baby having a built-in older brother to show him or her the ropes in life. Or to protect him or her from bullies, or to share ghost stories with when they made sheet-tents in the dark.

In my wheeling and dealing with the universe, I'd made a pledge to never be happy, to never have other children and to never get married, so that I could atone for my sins forever. In my vivid imagination, I had whittled the image of the five-hundred pound, chain-smoking me down to a neurotic, thin me with just one poor *lonely* child.

I mentioned I was a lot on the melodramatic side, right?

Giving my baby an older sibling was a bonus, so far as I could tell—he or she would never be lonely. I read the family bio, and my heart skipped erratically. *They liked vacationing on the Oregon coast.*

"I love the beach!" My stomach tensed with excitement—or Braxton Hicks.

They liked to go camping.

"Remember that time I went camping with Aunt Vickie and Uncle Paul? That was so much fun." Goose bumps raced up my spine.

"They've got a huge family." Satisfaction settled across my shoulders.

The more I stared at the color photo, the more I read about these fabulous people—-Dee was a teacher, and Garth worked at the hospital—I knew that I'd found exactly what I'd been hoping for.

"I want them."

My mom and Mrs. J. laughed. The wonderful, miracle-working lawyer got up off the edge of the chair. "Okay then.

I'll set up a meeting as soon as possible."

"I'm ready whenever they are."

Sighing with relief, I sat back. This was one of those rare moments when I knew everything would be all right.

Meeting the Arkell family was a brilliant spot in a scary time. Our first meeting was at a park, and Ricky came too.

We wanted to keep things neutral and meet in a safe place for all of us. It was strange, and I wore my attitude on my sleeve despite the warm, late-spring weather.

I took defensive behavior to another level—these people had the power to change my life. But it didn't take long to see that they were as wonderful in person as they seemed from their picture.

They were a family.

Another time, they came to our house to meet. My mom said that she was impressed with how gentle they were with their son. Loren really liked them, too.

During one of my over-analyzing binges, I remember trying to figure out how they would fit into my life—into all of our lives—if I let them in.

Would I have a place in theirs?

We didn't talk particulars at first. We kept things short and sweet, sort of like a reconnaissance mission, where we each used super-sensory antennae to see if we were compatible.

We were.

I knew it—I'd known it from just looking at their picture—but getting to know them in person cemented the fact that they were Just Right.

They took a big emotional chance, bringing their son Pat with them, letting him be a part of whatever was happening. But that was just the type of people they were, open, honest and innately generous.

They were curious about me, about how I'd ended up in the situation I was in. They didn't pry or ask questions that might have been too personal.

I used my very false bravado to exude a self-confidence that I didn't really feel. I didn't know any other way to be.

At the time, Ricky and I were still trying to sort things out, to see if we had a chance at anything other than 'friends,' but we weren't comfortable with each other and it was obvious.

I explained to Dee and Garth about the one night of teenaged passion in Seattle and about how Ricky and I were sort of together, but not really.

I was hoping to be clear that I wasn't interested in teen marriage or single parenting. I loved my baby (we found out we were having a boy!) and wanted the world for him.

Dee and Garth were cool with everything, and completely non-judgmental. They seemed like the kind of people who would roll with the trouble life randomly tossed at everybody. Divorce wasn't an option for them. They were committed to each other and their family.

We decided that we'd set up a post office box for correspondence. Dee would prove to be better at that than I was. She meant every word she ever told me. When I asked if she would be able to send pictures—not all the time, but of the important stuff—she readily agreed.

I wasn't sure how much I wanted to be involved, and she and Garth were really great about that. I didn't know if it would be better for my personal sanity to disappear off the face of the earth for a while, or to hang around on the periphery of their world.

Door Half Closed

The more I got to know Dee and Garth, the more I knew that this was the best choice—the end of a bad string of choices I'd made. They were my hope for the future, though I don't think they ever knew it.

We spent the next three months making the occasional visits. Ricky met them twice, but he had such a difficult time with the entire situation, that he opted out after that.

Which ridiculously hurt my feelings. After all, he'd said he wanted to be there for me, for his baby, too, but when it got emotionally tough, he bailed.

He still went out and partied. He still got to be skinny and hang out at the park. It was a bitter pill to swallow, but I'd let him off the hook months ago, allowing him to do what he wanted. What he wanted was to hang out, drink and be cool. We had nothing left in common.

That hurt too.

There were times when I felt like I'd been pregnant forever and ever and ever.

My due date was August 17. On August 16, I was too tired to make the graduation ceremony for my trade-school degree. For the first time in months, my stomach wasn't queasy, and I ate salad and lasagna for dinner.

I watched television with my folks and complained about a new backache.

After an hour, my mom noticed that my backaches were coming ten minutes apart.

I naively told her that I wasn't due for another day, as if a circled date on a calendar could dictate to mother nature.

We went to the hospital at midnight, and I had my baby boy at three in the morning. All natural, just like I'd wanted. There's something to be said for not knowing what was going to happen—I couldn't be afraid of it.

Door Half Closed

My mom was there with me, and it was over before I knew it.

I had a healthy 7 lb. 9 oz. baby boy. Dee and Garth had chosen to name him Kasey. It was my 'birth plan' to keep him with me for the first forty-eight hours, until I was released from the hospital.

It was selfish, and I acknowledged it, but I wanted those first two days with him, so that Kasey could know how much he was loved by me, my family and my friends. Bonnie, Susie, Michelle, Carrie and Dan were all there.

We couldn't get a hold of Ricky until later. My little brother, my stepsister, my mom and Loren–they were all there. That baby was adored and time was precious, because I knew that at the end of the forty-eight hours, I would be handing him over to his real life.

My place, my role, was mostly finished. I'd carried him to term, taken him to shows, fed him chili and mashed potatoes, and snuggled with him and our kitten. We'd gone on scooter rides, we'd thought a lot about our place in the world.

He'd kept me from being too lonely while I'd waited for him to be born. I'd spent hours rubbing my belly, promising to always love him, and to always be honest with him about the adoption.

I worried that he'd grow up and hate me.

I spent those forty-eight hours saying good-bye to my nine-month long roommate, to the heart that beat beneath my heart. Would he remember? Would it be better if he didn't remember?

What if I was making another mistake—not by the adoption, but by demanding an open adoption? What if people kept it secret for a reason?

But I couldn't.

Kasey was an innocent baby, who deserved truth and love and happiness, not dark, hushed-up secrets.

My prayer, and yes, I prayed, was that he would know how much I agonized over the decision to give him to a family who could care for him way better than I could.

I promised that no matter how tough it would be, I would always talk to him, or answer his questions.

Those forty-eight hours were mine, and I cherished them.

We called Dee and Garth so they could see their healthy baby boy for a quick visit, and then they respected my request for privacy until it was time to hand him over.

I found out later that they snuck into the hospital with a camera, but I don't blame them. I probably would have done the same!

The nurses and the doctor were all adamant that I could keep my baby, that nobody could take him from me if I changed my mind.

It was tempting in that very tiniest part of me that had wondered what it would be like to be a mom—even a not so good one. That selfish part of my psyche that urged me to cut and run.

I squished that voice down, because I'd already made the right decision, I'd chosen parents for Kasey that any child would be lucky to have. He would have a family that was prepared to love him and provide for him and protect him.

I could love him, which I did—I never stopped loving Kasey—but I couldn't protect him from the realities of what our world would have been.

Once this chapter of my life was done, I'd need to figure things out and make sure I was never in this situation again.

For the moment, I made sure to kiss all of Kasey's fingers and toes and to hold him as often as I could.

The doctors weren't sure that this was the best idea, not if I was really going to go through with the adoption, but I knew what I needed to do if I were to have no regrets.

My family supported that decision, and the doctor and nurses had to back down.

I didn't want pain pills or antidepressants, I wanted to feel and accept the pain of loss mixed with hope for the future. I would be living with that emotion for a long time, and I had to know what it was so that I could identify it and put it away. Contrary to what the doctor worried about, I understood—thanks to all of that soul-searching—exactly what I was losing.

And what I'd gained.

My baby would never go hungry, or lack medical attention or dental care. He would have a life that wasn't living hand to mouth, eating peanut butter and macaroni and bulk cheese. He wouldn't have to grow up with a worried, angry-at-the world mom.

His life would be good.

When those forty-eight hours were over and I'd kissed his head for the last time, I swore that I'd be fine. I relied on my tough chick persona to get me out of the hospital without turning into a nutcase.

Crying had gotten me nowhere, and I had to face whatever tomorrow would bring with dignity and self-respect. I'd promised Kasey.

What happened next was bizarre. I said my tearful and painful good-byes. I went home, knowing that Dee and Garth and Pat would take Kasey home and start their life.

But then the hospital wouldn't let Dee and Garth take Kasey home.

It was a Sunday evening. The hospital staff was going to keep Kasey in the hospital—alone—for another night at least. Who knew when the paperwork would be finished and Dee and Garth could get Kasey.

The whole idea of what we'd done was to make it so that Kasey would always be with people who loved him—not strangers in a nursery.

Dee and Garth called me, and after they told me the problem, we decided that they should pick me up to go to the hospital with them so that I could sign Kasey out.

Legally, I had every right to take my child.

We talked to the hospital officials. The nurse and staff tried to talk us out of it. Repercussions for Dee and Garth, if I decided to keep Kasey and run, were huge—they had no legal right to Kasey.

They had to trust me.

I had already placed my trust in them, so I told the nurse to get Kasey ready, and that I would sign him out. Then I would give Kasey to Dee and Garth to take home, as we'd planned.

Everybody on staff knew we'd had this plan in place, so why this didn't go smoothly, I don't know.

It could have been a horrible thing.

Thanks to my protective emotional armor, I was able to ignore my broken heart and take Kasey into my arms again.

He wasn't mine to keep.

"Here's your baby boy," I whispered as I handed him over.

Rhonda Pollero

CHAPTER SIX
Life After Adoption

She's Adopted? I Keep Forgetting That

I don't know when it happened, but at some point a year or two after Katie came to live with us, I stopped thinking of her as my adopted daughter. She was my daughter. Period. Maybe because a weird thing happened. We'd adopted a brown-haired, green-eyed child, yet she'd morphed into a blonde, so we actually look alike. While that was never a great motivator for me when we were making our decision, it does eliminate the rude questions adoptive parents often suffer when out in public with a child who is visually different from the parent. I have a friend who adopted from China, and it never ceases to amaze me how many people just blurt out, "He/She's adopted, right?"

With Katie, I've experienced this to some degree. People would say, "She's adopted? Does she know?" Well, since Katie would be standing next to me when the person asked, it was a good thing we never kept it a secret. The other question that makes my jaw clench came often when Katie went through a phase where she'd tell any stranger within earshot that she was adopted. "Really?" the stranger would ask. "From Russia? What's wrong with her? I know most kids adopted outside of the country have problems."

I usually wanted to slap any idiot insensitive enough to

make that kind of statement in front of a child. Does Katie have some problems? Sure. She needed speech therapy, because the Cyrillic alphabet has thirty-five characters and several vowel sounds were not part of the English language. 'R' blends and certain vowel combinations were difficult for her to articulate. The other four kids in her speech therapy class were all native born and working to overcome lisps, stammering and any number of other speech problems. Geography doesn't seem to play a part in speech development.

Yes, her birth mother drank heavily, and she had no prenatal care. Fetal alcohol syndrome is a spectrum, and the effects on Katie are minimal and have been addressed by a little extra help with schoolwork.

Possibly the most prominent issue has been her teeth. Because of the lack of prenatal care and years of malnutrition, she has no enamel on her teeth. So, like many other twelve year olds, she has bonding on her teeth and will spend time in braces. But as I look around at her peer group, braces seem to be the norm rather than the exception.

I don't look at her and see my adopted daughter, I just see Katie.

Traci Hall

CHAPTER SIX
Life After Adoption

What life?

I am the proud owner of a lock of Kasey's hair, finger-prints in bright red paint and letters from Dee, along with pictures of a gap-toothed grin, and a chocolate smile over a first-year birthday cake.

Dee did everything she ever told me she would—and then some. I loved that she included the family in her pictures, because it gave me a glimpse into their world.

My baby was happy.

That first year after Kasey was born is sort of foggy. I had a certificate that said I was qualified for something other than preparing and/or serving fast food, and I got a job downtown at a florist shop.

I felt like a failure because I was no longer pregnant, and I still hadn't achieved the Pulitzer. Hadn't even sent in a story for submission.

It was too damn hard just surviving. Trying to decide if I liked who I was, after all of the cutting and trimming and prodding.

The problem was that even though I had changed, I didn't know what to do with the changes. Human beings are creatures of habit, and we tend to follow the path of least resistance. It's easier, that's why.

But I knew that if I didn't get out of Spokane soon, I would never leave. I might even settle for be prepping rose vases and making FTD specified floral designs for the rest of my life.

Now instead of feeling physically trapped by my own body, I felt bound by external circumstance.

My same group of friends hung out, drank beer, talked and had sex (except for me—my recent experience had given me an invisible, unbreakable chastity belt, and I was better guarded than Fort Knox).

Talking was getting me nowhere! How would I ever be great at anything if I didn't see something besides the mountains in Spokane? Or wait, even the mountains in Seattle? I wanted more.

The kids coming up from the scene were silly and young. I had no desire to hang out with a band just for the sake of listening to them guzzle beer, burp and tell outrageous lies about things they'd done or were gonna do.

And the people I did hear, the ones who weren't shouting, had horror stories of their own. People my age were dying–stupidly.

Taking acid and deciding to take a road trip isn't fun—it's a way to flip your car, break your neck, and die. Getting super drunk and stoned and going for a swim isn't a way to get sober—it's a way to drown.

Shooting heroine for deeper meaning is just suicide.

Maybe those people were searching, too, I didn't want to be like them.

There was a rage that filled me, an anger that would flame through my system like a wildfire out of control, and I didn't know where to direct it—other than toward my really dark stories. I'll give you the theme for them all: A band, a really screwed-up couple, and then death for both main characters. And sometimes I killed off everybody…depending on my mood.

It made me feel better.

I wrote notebooks and notebooks full of angsty stuff that helped me control my inner, unnamed fury.

I realize now that I needed a purpose, and back then I just couldn't accept that my destiny was in Spokane, Washington. Technically, I was born in Seattle, but I lived in Spokane, and the only "Greats" to come out of there were Bing Crosby and Gonzaga.

That spring, I moved to my aunt and uncle's house in California. They deserve Sainthood for taking in a nineteen-year-old, hormonal nightmare of a niece trying to make her way through the fog.

I decided I would be a singer.

I loved music, but I couldn't play an instrument to save my soul—no matter how much Dan had tried to teach me bass.

Tambourine? Not a problem. Two tambourines? I'm not coordinated enough for something in each hand.

If they'd had American Idol back then, I never would have dared to think that I could be good enough to make a living as a vocalist.

But as time passed, I started getting better at *life*. I wrote lyrics that weren't so filled with gloom and doom. My characters could have the occasional happy ending.

I met new friends, other people my age who partied. I was starting to wonder if there were any other kind? Although there were obvious differences, one being the way they dressed. Underground Punk wasn't cool. Anywhere.

The other notable difference in my new friends was they knew they had to have money.

Riverside California didn't have the bus system that Spokane did, and if you wanted to go somewhere, you had to have a car. A ten-dollar bus pass wasn't even an option, and neither was walking. Little cities were sprawled along the freeway, available only by vehicle.

I got a job selling perfume. I was given a box of designer knock-off scents and a territory to cover. I had to knock on every business door and give them our spiel. I'm not a big fan of perfume, and I never would have thought that I could sell a twenty-dollar bottle of the fake stuff, but I did okay.

That's where I met Greg, my future husband.

When Greg and I were given a promotion and a chance to go to Vegas and open a perfume office, we took it. I could sell perfume during the day, and sing at night.

I had visions of being on stage and belting out songs to a crowd of adoring fans. The night, the lights, the atmosphere in Vegas is glittery and wild—in the dark.

In the day, it was dirty and desperate.

I *hated* selling perfume. We weren't making money. I wanted to be successful so badly that it was an ache in my chest.

And again, I was in with the same exact crowd that I'd been in with before. How had that happened?

I grabbed my courage and what was left of my self-respect and auditioned to be a singer. The lady was very cool and said she could start me right away as a back-up singer.

I've never been able to lie to myself. I read between the lines. I was good, but I wasn't good enough. Thanks to *American Idol*, I know now what kind of talent is out there in the world, and no way could I compete.

But no way was I going to settle for being a back-up singer for the rest of my life.

Was this being true to the months of soul searching with which I'd tortured myself? Not even close.

A light bulb flickered over my head, and I saw very clearly that I was chasing my own tail, making the same mistakes, only in a different State.

It wouldn't matter where I lived if I didn't choose something and work at it. I knew that dreams were intangible things that might not ever make money. Being a back-up singer might be fun now, but when I was thirty?

Ugh.

Being a writer didn't pay unless you were a 'big name.' I didn't have a formal education in literature to give me a boost toward a literary career.

I needed a real job. It was time, in my mind, for me to put the dreams away and grow up.

Greg was awesome about my moment of Zen. I told him what I needed, which was to quit the late-night scene and stop running from myself. I loved him, but I understood if he wasn't in the same place as me. Our future together—if we stayed together—would have to be very different from our partying past. I was terrified he would say no, but I knew that either way I had to leave.

He agreed to give up the party scene and drive to Spokane with me, and we've been together ever since. He's been the one man—the one *person*—in my life who knows me, scars and all.

After twenty years, I know he still loves me, and that's always been the best balm for my heart.

We were twenty and twenty-one when we arrived in Spokane that January, totally committed to one another.

I finally understood that life is about having the courage to take the next step, one foot after the other. Sometimes you trip, but you gotta keep on going, scabby knees and all.

Greg has always been great about Kasey. He thought it was incredible that Dee and Garth were so open about their lives with Kasey.

We were lucky because they would occasionally bring Kasey by, maybe once a year? At first, he terrified me.

He had blond, blond hair and a happy grin. His eyes twinkled so brightly and he looked like my little brother. *Did he hate me yet?*

Greg would play with Kasey, get right down on the floor and wrestle. I don't know what I was afraid of…maybe of being happy.

How did I deserve being happy? Hadn't I done the most awful thing a mother could do? I'd deliberately chosen open adoption so that there would be no secrets.

Now I understood why anonymity might be a good thing.

I thought I had an idea of what seeing Kasey grow up would be like, but the reality was that with each toddler laugh, with each smile, it felt like tearing a scab off a wound that had never really healed.

He wasn't mine to hold, but I was so grateful for the chance to see that he was cherished. Dee, Garth and Patrick—and all of their extended family—had made my baby theirs to love, and it was exactly what I'd wanted.

I could live with the ache. Greg and my family were always there to put on another bandage after the visits.

Time made things easier. Greg and I got married. The weird thing was that when I got pregnant, I felt like I was betraying Kasey's memory.

I worked in an office (who knew I could be a secretary and handle ten phone lines? This job had insurance, for pete's sake) and another girl, Sarah, was also pregnant.

Greg and I did everything by the book. No way was I going to mess around with this pregnancy. I treated it like it was 'serious business.' What was I thinking?? I knew I couldn't be a mother.

Sarah had her baby two weeks before me, and she brought her bundle of joy into the office breakroom. Everybody was cooing and awing and wanting to hold her.

I had tears in my eyes and my arms weren't just trembling, they were shaking as if I was possessed. I knew that I would be a failure as a mom—especially if I couldn't hold my baby!

Telling Greg we were in big trouble, he somehow managed to calm my fears.

I was convinced that somehow I hadn't gotten the maternal gene. I'd given a child up for adoption—that made me a pariah, a loser—certainly not a woman who should have the chance to try again.

I was fooling myself! Thinking I could ever be good at this one thing.

Reading baby book after baby book, I went to all kinds of classes, and Greg and I practiced the breathing together. I ate, even though I was so freaking sick. I ate for that baby inside me. I put on seventy pounds of Kentucky-Fried-Chicken weight, just to make sure he was healthy.

We knew we were having a boy.

Kasey, in case I'd forgotten, was a boy.

I remained a queen of the what-if game, only now I played it with my mom and Greg.

Me: What if this baby hates me, too?

My mom: If you say that one more time, I'm hanging up the phone.

Greg: Kasey isn't going to hate you. This baby will only hate you if you make him eat his vegetables.

Me: We need to buy a blender.

Overwhelmed by the end of my pregnancy, I pushed all doubt aside so that I could concentrate on being the best mom I could—which, thanks to all of my reading, meant that I could do infant CPR and puree baby food.

I would make mistakes, but my child would never doubt that I loved him.

Bringing Brighton into the world was so much different than my experience with Kasey… I had a husband who was thrilled to be there at Brighton's birth, and he'd been my partner in the breathing-during-contractions ordeal.

I still had a thing against the epidural.

We had a birthing suite, a car seat to take our baby home in, and a little outfit for Brighton to wear. Although, since Brighton was almost nine pounds (blame it on the potatoes!), we had to get something else for him to wear.

It was a beautiful experience. I couldn't let the guilt stay. It didn't belong inside me anymore.

I was able to hold Brighton without dropping him, which felt like my first success.

So we did it again, and this time we had a girl.

Brighton was blond, like Kasey. They had similarities, but it was my daughter, Destini, who really looked like Kasey.

Greg and I talked it over, and we wanted our kids to

know that they had an older half brother. We talked to Dee and Garth about it, and they agreed that it would be the natural evolution of things.

We explained to our kids that Kasey had a different daddy than Brighton and Destini—it was always a fact and there was nothing icky about it. No ugly secrets. It was the truth, and wouldn't require more explanation until later— but by then, Kasey was a part of their lives, too.

We took pictures of the three of them together, and it was easy to see they were related. Kasey's older brother, Patrick, was there for my two, also. He would play with Brighton and Destini, carrying them around on his shoulders until they squealed. Especially Destini, who liked being flown across the room like an airplane.

Dee and Garth treated my kids like an extension of their family, and that's what we became.

After Greg and I moved back to Spokane from Seattle, we lived less than a mile away from Dee and Garth, although we didn't know it at the time.

I think that our open adoption was successful, because we were all willing to be vulnerable. For Kasey's sake. He was being raised by two parents who loved him—he had an older brother who teased him and adored him—but we were there, in case he was ever interested.

I remember that Kasey must have been around eleven when I got a phone call from Dee, asking if I'd been drinking while I was pregnant. Shocked, I said, "Of course not." I'd been too sick to drink anything besides Sprite.

I can only imagine what a hard phone call that was for her to make, but Kasey was getting into some trouble at elementary school, and the teacher or guidance counselor had found out that Kasey was adopted.

And then proceeded to tell Dee and Garth that Kasey was suffering from Fetal Alcohol Syndrome.

Some professionals should keep their uneducated opinions to themselves. That person was looking to blame someone for Kasey's typical rebellious behavior. This was at a time when teachers were quick to tell parents that their kids were ADD or ADHD and that they would need medication before being accepted back into the classroom.

After being embarrassed that Dee would even have to ask such a question—but how else would she know?—I was happy to set the record straight. And thank God that we had the kind of relationship where I was just a phone call away.

That teacher or guidance counselor had made a quick judgment without knowing all the facts, without knowing me.

At this point in my employment history—I took jobs that allowed me to be home when my kids were home—I worked in the school district as a paraprofessional, and my specialty was working with the special needs behavior kids. There is a world of difference between boyish rebellion and a serious medical problem.

Another time, Kasey took off from school, and Garth came by our house to see if we had him. That was scary, but we made it very clear that if Kasey did come to us, we would be on the phone to them immediately.

Kasey was not my child to raise, as much as I loved him.

I think it turned out that he'd gone to a friend's house, but we—our two families—were respecting the agreement we'd made. To be open, honest and available—even when it wasn't easy. But this is why it worked.

We'd get all of the kids together at Christmas and in the summer for birthdays. Of the four kids, Brighton was the only winter baby, and he liked getting a gift midyear!

As the kids got older, we followed their lead. Kasey came over to our house when we had 'Santa'—grandpa in a Santa suit—visit.

We'd bump into each other around town. My grandma swam with Dee's mom down at the YMCA. For a time, we all went to the same church as Dee's sister. Often, Greg and Garth would take the boys and go play roller hockey under the freeway.

I realized our families were meant to be entwined, but the frosting on the 'fate cake' was when Dee's niece married my cousin, and we all went to the same wedding.

There is no such thing as a perfect family. There are blended families, integrated families, extended families, unrelated families, patchwork families—it doesn't matter. Family is comprised of the people in your life, and Kasey, thanks to Dee and Garth, is in my family.

I couldn't be luckier.

Rhonda Pollero

CHAPTER SEVEN

In the End

A Look Back at the Last Ten Years

Okay, so my life took some unexpected, difficult and bittersweet turns. I thought by now I'd be hating whatever girl my son was dating; after all, no one would have been good enough for my son. He'd be out of college, and I'd have had an empty nest. Bob would have retired, and we'd be living in Florida. Florida, because my husband is a native New Yorker, and I think they are legally required to move to Florida once they retire.

I never thought I'd be driving car pools at fifty. I didn't think I'd be attending dance recitals and middle-school awards ceremonies. I thought by now the annoyance of annual Science Fair projects would be little more than unpleasant memories.

Bob did retire, and we did move to Florida. The good thing about being a writer is I can do my job anywhere. The mandatory move to Florida has been good. I like living near the ocean, and Katie has settled into life split between school and dance. She's a stunning and—for her age—accomplished dancer.

She is also, I'm told, a mini-me. Yes, we have tween drama from time to time but, for the most part, we have a great relationship. She's a happy kid. She is spoiled, but then again, she's an only child, so that's not any great shock. I don't mind that she's spoiled, so long as she isn't rude. So what if she has a lot of stuff? What matters is that she has a sense of security and knows she is loved unconditionally.

Katie enjoys the time she gets to spend with her older siblings and their families. She's an aunt to a girl five years older than she is, as well as a niece five years younger and twins who are eight years her junior. Is it a typical family? No, but what is a typical family these days?

Our ever-growing extended family has, for the most part, embraced Katie, and the fact that she's adopted seems to have faded away. Yes, we have one relative who continues to find fault, voicing ridiculous thoughts like, "She's tall, so they must have lied about her age." Maybe she's tall because she had tall birth parents. I don't really care. Physically, she'll be what she'll be.

I'm often asked how I'll feel if she decides to search out her birth family. I'm fine with it. I think if I was adopted, I would be curious, too. I'm not threatened by the possibility. I am absolutely secure in my role as her mother, and even if she does some day reconnect with her birth mother, my place in her life won't change.

I'm most proud of the fact that she's growing up knowing about Kyle, but not living in his shadow. On his birthday and the anniversary of his death, she gives us extra hugs and kisses, because she knows those are difficult days for us.

The other 363 days, her attention is on things like clothes, hair, what kind of car she'll get when she turns sixteen and if she'll earn a solo part in the next dance production. Like every other almost twelve year old, she claims to be the only kid suffering day in and day out because she doesn't have an iPhone. Or because everyone has been to Europe but her. Or because there's a boy in her class who she likes one week and can't tolerate seven days later. Oh, and her laptop is old, so she really *needs* another one.

Have I made some parental missteps? Sure. Because of Kyle's death, Katie gets dragged to the doctor for every cough and sniffle. Luckily, I have a doctor who understands my parental neuroses and placates my overreaction. I'm probably a tad overprotective. I need to know where she is and whom she's with at all times.

Parenting any child is an eighteen- to twenty-year crap-shoot. You never know until they leave home for good whether you've given them the tools and the moral compass to navigate life on their own.

Traci Hall

CHAPTER SEVEN
In the End

Happily Ever After
Twenty-Two Years Later

Greg and I moved to Florida when the kids were ten and twelve. I'd spent all my young adult life wanting to escape Spokane, and suddenly I was leaving.

I didn't want to go.

The roots I'd fought so hard against putting down were firmly entrenched in the Pacific Northwest. Greg and I would tell his family in California that we enjoyed having four seasons, compared to California's two.

Arizona? Ha. Only one season there, and it was hot.

We'd made a life for ourselves that centered around family, friends, and work. Greg and I had come a long way from the aimlessness of the party scene.

I was afraid of leaving everyone. I was scared for my kids—what would they do without Grandma and Grandpa? Uncle Jim? Gigi? Grandma Maria? With all of the numerous aunts and uncles and cousins, we were a clan.

We'd grown close to Dee and Garth, Kasey and Pat. I was thrilled when Kasey got to come and spend some time with us in our new townhouse in Florida.

In the End

It was awe inspiring to see how much better he had his life together than I'd ever had mine!

Kasey's a cool person. Funny, charming, cute—of course—and easy to be with.

He didn't hate me.

I tried to be open to whatever questions he might have had about me or Ricky, but he didn't really have any. He'd been curious a few years before about Ricky, and so I'd called Ricky's dad in Seattle.

I'd said I was an old friend. I'd never met Ricky's parents, and I didn't know if they knew about me—or Kasey, really.

Ricky's dad let me know in no uncertain terms that Ricky was out partying, that he lived with someone, and that he didn't need any more 'old' friends.

I didn't leave my name or number.

I'm sure my life now seemed normal to Kasey. Dee said that she and Garth told Kasey growing up that I'd loved him, but I just wasn't able to take care of him the way he needed to be cared for.

But here I was with two kids and a husband, a house and a life. I used to feel guilty for being happy.

Once Kasey turned eighteen, I let go of that for good.

He's a great person in his own right. Dee and Garth raised a young man any parent would be proud of.

I stay on the sidelines, grateful to have been given the glimpses into his life that I've gotten…because I took a risk, and chose open adoption.

You bet I'm proud.

Not long ago, Patrick got married to a beautiful young

lady. He's a daddy now—and a great one, according to his mom. I've seen the love in his face for his tiny daughter—in the picture, Kasey is cradling his niece in the crook of his arm.

Life goes full circle, and as I study the photo, I know I've seen Kasey's expression before. I dig out the old pictures I've saved, and I've got one of Ricky, holding Kasey.

It's déjà vu.

Once I can breathe again, I compare the pictures side by side.

There's a huge difference, now that I'm really looking.

Kasey is happy and confident while holding his niece to his heart—he knows his place in this baby's life.

Ricky is smiling, but uncertainty lies beneath the uplifting of his lips. He cares, but he doesn't quite understand what to do with the beautiful boy in his arms.

That boy turned out to be a terrific man, with everything we'd ever wished for him when we'd talked—before we stopped talking.

Kasey's content, in good health and he never doubted that he was loved.

Dee and I were on the phone last night, talking about this book and how far we've all come since we first met. How much we've changed.

She admitted that I'd had a bit of an attitude at the beginning. I laughed, telling her that I'd been afraid of being judged—people were quick to come to a conclusion of their own without knowing all of the facts.

It didn't help that my black nail polish was chipped and my hair rivaled that of the Flock of Seagulls.

My first reaction to anybody in those days was to snarl and hope that they'd leave me alone. I was tough, remember?

For me, giving into family and accepting love meant being vulnerable. If you show that soft white underbelly to the world, you could get gutted. Live life with your elbows out, and you'll never get hurt.

Uh huh.

I've softened up a lot since then. I had my reasons for being hard—and they were valid—but you can't live in the murky past.

I give thanks to the universe every day that I've grown into the person I am today. Life still throws the occasional screwball, and you have to duck fast or get smacked upside the head.

Having Kasey made me strong without the hardness. I learned to accept that pain is a fact of life, and it's not an excuse to stick your head in the sand.

Being pregnant with Kasey saved me from becoming another statistic. I knew that having Kasey would give me the chance to be something incredible.

It did.

I became a mother.

Even though he was not mine to bring up and provide a home for, I still loved him—always. I believe that open adoption alleviated the worry and concern that I might have had over the years.

Instead of regret, I got pictures of Kasey playing with his older brother Patrick on the coast of Oregon.

Instead of bitterness, I was given a lock of hair. I was never treated like I was unwelcome, and I was never shut out of Kasey's life.

I had the stretch marks to prove I'd born a child; however, that didn't make me Mom. But there was no denying the tug at my heart, or the sense that something vital might be missing.

Dee and Garth filled that void with letters. Not a lot of them, and it was never intrusive. It was just right, and those letters were so appreciated!

My part of the bargain was to live my life without looking back at what might have been.

No regrets.

Greg and I have a son and a daughter who are our world, just as Dee and Garth have Pat and Kasey at the center of theirs. I wouldn't change a thing.

And as funny as it seems, that includes getting pregnant in the first place.

Patrick is married and starting his own family. Kasey is working and dating and enjoying life. Brighton just graduated and is on his way to college. Destini graduates this year, then she'll go on to take her spot in the world.

I've been blessed.

Rhonda Pollero

I'm not sure I'd be a whole person today had it not been for the love and support Bob and I shared during the darkest and brightest moments in our lives. They say time heals all wounds, but that's pretty much crap. Time just makes it different. Sure, you can get through the day without crying, but that doesn't mean the grief of losing your child isn't with you every moment of every day.

Katie has been our joy, our challenge and our savior. She is a sweet child ninety percent of the time. The other ten percent her head is spinning on her shoulders. That's because she's standing on the precipice of the teenage years. She's no different than any of her friends, so I guess I can say she's a well-adapted, well-loved child.

I know I'm lucky. Foreign adoptions don't always work out. That's no one's fault. Unlike adopting out of the foster care system, where you get to spend time with the child prior to adopting, with a foreign adoption, the child is thrust into your arms. You're a stranger to them and they may never bond with you or vice versa. I was prepared by my agency, but had they not told me ahead of time that it could take Katie some time to warm up to me, I probably would have fallen to pieces.

Now I'm enjoying the milestones. Fifth grade graduation, dance recitals. All are happy occasions. I'm a little scared of how I'll feel when Katie achieves things Kyle never did–when she has a date, learns to drive, picks a college—all that will be new and unknown territory. But like most aspects of childrearing, there is no handbook, so I won't know what it will be like 'til I get there.

Traci Hall

Thank you to everybody in my life, most especially my mom—you let me be my own person and I'm forever grateful for that. I hope I've done the same for my kids! Aunt Vicki and Uncle Paul—thanks for accepting me into your home and hearts. Dee and Garth, I'm a writer, but your generosity and love has always left me at a loss for words. I hope this book helps explain my respect and appreciation for you.

To Patrick, and your endearing grin, and to Kasey, for being you!

To Brighton and Destini—you both fill my heart with love, and most importantly to Greg, who holds it all.

Editor's Note

From Bonnie Crisalli

I have to admit, I did feel a bit hypocritical editing a book entitled, *Adoption is Forever*, since my husband and I were adoptive parents…only it didn't turn out to be forever. In fact, our experience was similar to Rhonda's, in that we adopted a child from Russia; but then it turned out to be more like Traci's, since we wound up having to find the right family for the child.

Our experience was what is called a failed adoption, which you don't hear too much about, understandably so. It wouldn't do to discourage people from wanting to adopt, when there are so many kids who need good homes.

Briefly, our own experience began when our son, Nicholas, was five years old and we decided it was high time he had a sibling. We'd been trying to get pregnant for a couple years, but it wasn't happening, and I was reluctant to go the fertility-treatment route. We decided to adopt an older boy (closer to Nicholas's age) from Russia.

Everything went pretty smoothly with the adoption, though there were a lot of similarities with Rhonda's Russian experience. We brought home a three-year-old boy, Jackson, within four months of making our decision.

The situation seemed idyllic, until the day after we returned from Russia, and I was unpacking my bag. Hmmmm…why hadn't I used my tampons on our trip? I was supposed to have gotten my period while we were there. You guessed it, I was pregnant.

Now, in and of itself, this does not seem like it should have been a problem, but—to cut a long story short—a lot happened in the three years that we had Jackson. Our daughter, Samantha, was born eight months after we adopted Jackson. Things weren't too bad during the pregnancy, when I could pay a lot of attention to Jackson, but once Samantha arrived and I had to divide my attention…well, let's just say all hell broke loose—and that's putting it ridiculously mildly.

Eventually, Jackson was diagnosed with extreme ADHD, and it was the opinion of two different therapists that we should seriously consider finding a new home for Jackson. You see, the problem was that being a middle child was the worst possible scenario for a child like Jackson. He needed our attention to be focused on him 24/7, and would act up in any and every way to get that attention—any attention would do, negative or positive.

It was the most difficult decision we've ever had to make and, yes, it put a great strain on our marriage; but then so did living in a chaotic household for three years. Like Traci, we opted for an open adoption and did lots of research in order to find the perfect family for Jackson.

For six years now, Jackson has been with his second adoptive parents, a lovely, lovely couple, who actually requested a child with special needs. They have two older children from a previous marriage of the father, and the mother, an RN, could not have children of her own. So, Jackson wound up capturing the attention of four adults. When we met the four of them and watched them interact with Jackson, we knew immediately that they were the ones. And, much to Jackson's delight, they also had three dogs and a swimming pool!

Not to make light of this, it was still a very difficult decision. There are a lot of people who chose to judge us (not knowing anything about what we'd been through) for our

Editor's Note

decision, and to them we will always be 'that family who gave up a child for adoption.' In our hearts, we know we did the right thing for us—and especially for Jackson—and we have never once questioned whether we made the right decision. Our families and close friends stood by us unflinchingly, as they too knew it was the right thing.

We now have three children (Max came along, much to our surprise, four and a half years ago), and after some pretty severe rough patches, our marriage is back on track. Had we kept Jackson, I do not believe that we would still be married.

www.ingramcontent.com/pod-product-compliance
Lightning Source LLC
Chambersburg PA
CBHW072343100426
42736CB00044B/1893